United States Government Accountability Office

Report to Congressional Requesters

I0412192

September 2014

DATA CENTER CONSOLIDATION

Reporting Can Be Improved to Reflect Substantial Planned Savings

GAO Highlights

Highlights of GAO-14-713, a report to congressional requesters

DATA CENTER CONSOLIDATION

Reporting Can Be Improved to Reflect Substantial Planned Savings

Why GAO Did This Study

In 2010, as focal point for information technology management across the government, OMB's Federal Chief Information Officer launched the Federal Data Center Consolidation Initiative to consolidate the growing number of centers. As of May 2014, agencies reported a total of 9,658 data centers—approximately 6,500 more than reported by OMB in 2011.

GAO was asked to review federal agencies' continuing efforts to consolidate their data centers and achieve cost savings. The objectives were to (1) evaluate the extent to which agencies have achieved cost savings to date and identified future savings through their consolidation efforts, (2) identify agencies' notable consolidation successes and challenges in achieving cost savings, and (3) evaluate the extent to which data center optimization metrics have been established. GAO assessed agency-reported cost savings and avoidance documentation, interviewed agency officials, and assessed data center optimization metrics against prior OMB requirements and goals.

What GAO Recommends

GAO is recommending that OMB assist agencies in reporting cost savings and develop a metric for server utilization as part of any reevaluation of the metrics. GAO is also recommending, among other things, that agencies fully report their consolidation cost savings. OMB and 12 agencies agreed, 1 did not state whether it agreed or disagreed, 1 had no comments, and 1 partially agreed noting challenges. GAO continues to believe the recommendation remains valid as discussed in the report.

View GAO-14-713. For more information, contact David A. Powner at (202) 512-9286 or pownerd@gao.gov.

What GAO Found

Of the 24 agencies participating in the Federal Data Center Consolidation Initiative, 19 agencies collectively reported achieving an estimated $1.1 billion in cost savings and avoidances between fiscal years 2011 and 2013. Notably, the Departments of Defense, Homeland Security, and Treasury accounted for approximately $850 million (or 74 percent) of the total. In addition, 21 agencies collectively reported planning an additional $2.1 billion in cost savings and avoidances by the end of fiscal year 2015, for a total of approximately $3.3 billion—an amount that is about $300 million higher than the Office of Management and Budget's (OMB) original $3 billion goal. Between fiscal years 2011 and 2017, agencies reported planning a total of about $5.3 billion in cost savings and avoidances.

Agencies' Data Center Consolidation Cost Savings and Avoidances (Dollars in Millions)

Fiscal year	Estimated and actual			Planned				Total
	2011	2012	2013	2014	2015	2016	2017	
Total savings and avoidances	$192	$268	$683	$895	$1,250	$917	$1,144	$5,350
	$1,143 total			$4,206 total				

Source: GAO analysis of agency data. | GAO-14-713 Note: Totals may not add due to rounding.

However, planned savings may be higher because six agencies that reported having closed as many as 67 data centers reported limited or no savings, in part because they encountered difficulties, such as calculating baseline data center costs. In addition, 11 of the 21 agencies with planned cost savings are underreporting their fiscal years 2012 through 2015 figures to OMB by approximately $2.2 billion. While several agencies noted communication issues as the reason for this, others did not provide a reason. Until OMB assists agencies in reporting savings and agencies fully report their savings, the $5.3 billion in total savings will be understated.

Most agencies reported successes in achieving cost savings—notably, the benefits of key technologies, reduced power consumption and facility costs, and improvements in asset inventories. However, agencies also reported challenges, many of which were the same as GAO found in 2012. One of the most-reported challenges was related to obtaining power usage information as a means to determine cost savings. In light of how closely these successes and challenges relate to achieving cost savings, it is important for OMB to continue to provide leadership and guidance, including—as GAO previously recommended—using the Data Center Consolidation Task Force to monitor agencies' efforts.

Pursuant to OMB guidance, in May 2014 the Data Center Consolidation Task Force completed a set of 11 metrics to measure agency progress toward optimizing their data centers, such as power usage and facility utilization. In addition, related targets to be achieved by fiscal year 2015 have been developed for nearly all the metrics. However, the metrics do not address server utilization, even though OMB reported this to be as low as 5 percent in 2009, which is significantly below OMB's target of 60 to 70 percent. Without such a metric, OMB may not be getting important insight into agencies' progress on a key issue that was a driving factor in launching the consolidation initiative.

_____ United States Government Accountability Office

Contents

Figure

Abbreviations

CIO	chief information officer
DHS	Department of Homeland Security
EPA	Environmental Protection Agency
FDCCI	Federal Data Center Consolidation Initiative
GPRAMA	Government Performance and Results Act Modernization Act of 2010
GSA	General Services Administration
HHS	Department of Health and Human Services
HUD	Department of Housing and Urban Development
IT	information technology
NASA	National Aeronautics and Space Administration
NRC	Nuclear Regulatory Commission
NSF	National Science Foundation
OMB	Office of Management and Budget
OPM	Office of Personnel Management
SBA	Small Business Administration
SSA	Social Security Administration
Task Force	Data Center Consolidation Task Force
USAID	U.S. Agency for International Development
VA	Department of Veterans Affairs

GAO U.S. GOVERNMENT ACCOUNTABILITY OFFICE

441 G St. N.W.
Washington, DC 20548

September 25, 2014

Congressional Requesters

The federal government's demand for information technology (IT) is ever increasing. In recent years, as federal agencies have modernized their operations, put more of their services online, and increased their information security profiles, their need for computing power and data storage resources has increased. Over time, this increasing demand led to a dramatic rise in the number of federal data centers and a corresponding increase in operational costs. In response, the Office of Management and Budget's (OMB) Federal Chief Information Officer (CIO) launched the Federal Data Center Consolidation Initiative (FDCCI) in 2010.

During the past several years, we reported[1] and testified[2] that, while data center consolidation could potentially save the federal government billions of dollars, weaknesses existed in the execution and oversight of the initiative. Specifically, in July 2011 and July 2012, we reported that nearly

---

[1]GAO, *Data Center Consolidation: Strengthened Oversight Needed to Achieve Cost Savings Goal*, GAO-13-378 (Washington, D.C.: Apr. 23, 2013); *Data Center Consolidation: Agencies Making Progress on Efforts, but Inventories and Plans Need to Be Completed*, GAO-12-742 (Washington, D.C.: July 19, 2012); and *Data Center Consolidation: Agencies Need to Complete Inventories and Plans to Achieve Expected Savings*, GAO-11-565 (Washington, D.C.: July 19, 2011).

[2]GAO, *Information Technology: Reform Initiatives Can Help Improve Efficiency and Effectiveness*, GAO-14-671T (Washington, D.C.: June 10, 2014); *Information Technology: Implementing Best Practices and Reform Initiatives Can Help Improve the Management of Investments*, GAO-14-596T (Washington, D.C.: May 8, 2014); *Information Technology: OMB and Agencies Need to More Effectively Implement Major Initiatives to Save Billions of Dollars*, GAO-13-796T (Washington, D.C.: July 25, 2013); *Information Technology: OMB and Agencies Need to Focus Continued Attention on Eliminating Duplicative Investments*, GAO-13-685T (Washington, D.C.: June 11, 2013); and *Data Center Consolidation: Strengthened Oversight Needed to Achieve Billions of Dollars in Savings*, GAO-13-627T (Washington, D.C.: May 14, 2013).

GAO-14-713 Data Center Consolidation

all of the 24 departments and agencies (agencies) participating in FDCCI[3] had not yet completed a data center inventory or the consolidation plans to implement their consolidation initiative. More recently, in April 2013, we found that OMB's oversight of the initiative had shortcomings, including that the agency was not tracking and reporting cost savings. As a result, we recommended that OMB require agencies to complete their missing inventory and plan elements and improve the execution of important oversight responsibilities, among other things. Subsequently, OMB and agencies took actions to address these deficiencies, which are discussed later in this report.

Given the importance of the consolidation initiative, you asked that we review federal agencies' continuing efforts to consolidate their data centers and achieve cost savings. Specifically, our objectives were to (1) evaluate the extent to which agencies have achieved cost savings to date and identified future savings through their consolidation efforts, (2) identify agencies' notable consolidation successes and challenges in achieving cost savings, and (3) evaluate the extent to which data center optimization metrics have been established.

To address our first objective, we obtained and analyzed the 24 FDCCI agencies' cost savings and avoidance documentation, such as cost models, budget and contract documentation, and quarterly status reports to OMB. Then, we identified the total agency-reported savings achieved from fiscal years 2011 to 2013 and planned from fiscal years 2014 through 2017. We also compared agency documentation to data center consolidation cost savings and avoidance reporting requirements outlined in a March 2013 OMB memorandum.[4] To address our second objective, we reviewed all 24 agencies' documentation and interviewed agency officials to determine what consolidation successes have been realized in achieving cost savings and what challenges have been faced in achieving

---

[3]The 24 major departments and agencies that participate in FDCCI are the Departments of Agriculture, Commerce, Defense, Education, Energy, Health and Human Services, Homeland Security, Housing and Urban Development, the Interior, Justice, Labor, State, Transportation, the Treasury, and Veterans Affairs; the Environmental Protection Agency, General Services Administration, National Aeronautics and Space Administration, National Science Foundation, Nuclear Regulatory Commission, Office of Personnel Management, Small Business Administration, Social Security Administration, and U.S. Agency for International Development.

[4]OMB, *Fiscal Year 2013 PortfolioStat Guidance: Strengthening Federal IT Portfolio Management*, Memorandum M-13-09 (Washington, D.C.: Mar. 27, 2013).

cost savings. Finally, for our third objective, we compared the established data center optimization metrics to the requirements for such metrics, as documented in OMB's March 2013 memorandum,[5] and interviewed OMB, General Services Administration (GSA), and Data Center Consolidation Task Force (Task Force) officials to discuss the process by which the metrics were established and to determine the extent to which related targets for the metrics had been established. We also compared the established metrics against areas identified by OMB in prior data center consolidation-related memorandums and guidance as having importance to data center optimization.

We conducted this performance audit from October 2013 to September 2014 in accordance with generally accepted government auditing standards. Those standards require that we plan and perform the audit to obtain sufficient, appropriate evidence to provide a reasonable basis for our findings and conclusions based on our audit objectives. We believe that the evidence obtained provides a reasonable basis for our findings and conclusions based on our audit objectives. Appendix I contains further details about our objectives, scope, and methodology.

Background

The federal government's increasing demand for IT led to a dramatic rise in the number of federal data centers and a corresponding increase in operational costs. According to OMB, the federal government had 432 data centers in 1998 and more than 1,100 in 2009. Operating such a large number of centers has been and continues to be a significant cost to the federal government, including costs for hardware, software, real estate, and cooling. For example, in 2007, the Environmental Protection Agency (EPA) estimated that the electricity cost to operate federal servers and data centers across the government was about $450 million annually. According to the Department of Energy (Energy), data center spaces can consume 100 to 200 times more electricity than a standard office space. In 2009, OMB reported[6] that server utilization rates as low as 5 percent across the federal government's estimated 150,000 servers were a driving factor in the need to establish a coordinated, government-

---

[5]OMB, Memorandum M-13-09.

[6]OMB, *Inventory of Federal Data Center Activity*, Budget Data Request No. 09-41 (Washington, D.C.: Aug. 10, 2009).

wide effort to improve the efficiency, performance, and environmental footprint of federal data center activities.

OMB and the Federal CIO Established the Federal Data Center Consolidation Initiative

Concerned about the size of the federal data center inventory and the potential to improve the efficiency, performance, and the environmental footprint of federal data center activities, OMB, under the direction of the Federal CIO, established FDCCI in February 2010. This initiative's four high-level goals are to

- promote the use of "green IT"[7] by reducing the overall energy and real estate footprint of government data centers;

- reduce the cost of data center hardware, software, and operations;

- increase the overall IT security posture of the government; and

- shift IT investments to more efficient computing platforms and technologies.

As part of FDCCI, OMB required the 24 agencies to identify a data center consolidation program manager to lead the agency's consolidation efforts. In addition, agencies were required to submit an asset inventory baseline and other documents that would result in a plan for consolidating their data centers. The asset inventory baseline was to contain detailed information on each data center and identify the consolidation approach to be taken for each one. It would serve as the foundation for developing the final data center consolidation plan. The data center consolidation plan would serve as a technical road map and approach for achieving the targets for infrastructure utilization, energy efficiency, and cost efficiency and was to be incorporated into the agency's fiscal year 2012 budget.

In October 2010, OMB reported that all of the agencies had submitted an inventory and plan. In addition, in a series of memorandums, OMB described plans to monitor agencies' consolidation activities on an ongoing basis. Starting in fiscal year 2011, OMB required agencies to provide an updated data center asset inventory at the end of every third

---

[7]"Green IT" refers to environmentally sound computing practices that can include a variety of efforts, such as using energy-efficient data centers, purchasing computers that meet certain environmental standards, and recycling obsolete electronics.

quarter and an updated consolidation plan (including any missing elements) at the end of every fourth quarter. Further, starting in fiscal year 2012, OMB required agencies to provide a consolidation progress report at the end of every quarter. This progress information has subsequently been made available on the federal website dedicated to providing the public with access to datasets developed by federal agencies, http://data.gov.

Pursuant to requirements of the Government Performance and Results Act Modernization Act of 2010 (GPRAMA),[8] in February 2012, OMB designated data center consolidation as 1 of its 14 priority goals (now known as cross-agency priority goals) because of its importance to improving management across the federal government. These goals are designed to cover areas where increased cross-agency collaboration is needed to improve progress towards the achievement of goals shared by multiple contributing agencies. In March 2014, OMB announced the creation of a new set of goals in its submission of the President's fiscal year 2015 budget, which did not include data center consolidation. According to OMB, although the updated set of goals did not include the data center consolidation goal because it had reached the end of its goal cycle time frame under GPRAMA, the effort will remain an administration priority.

While OMB is primarily responsible for FDCCI, the agency designated the Federal CIO Council—the principal interagency forum to improve IT-related practices across the federal government—to lead the effort. In addition, OMB originally identified two additional organizations to assist in managing and overseeing the initiative:

- The GSA FDCCI Program Management Office to support OMB in planning, execution, management, and communications.

- The Task Force is comprised of the data center consolidation program managers from each agency. According to its charter, the Task Force is critical to supporting collaboration across agencies, including identifying and disseminating key information, solutions, and processes that will help agencies in their consolidation efforts.

---

[8]Pub. L. No. 111-352, 124 Stat. 3866 (Jan. 4, 2011). GPRAMA significantly enhanced the Government Performance and Results Act of 1993, Pub. L. No. 103-62, 107 Stat. 285 (Aug. 3, 1993).

However, in December 2013, GSA and Task Force officials stated that the GSA's Program Management Office would no longer be supporting FDCCI and its responsibilities were being transitioned to OMB and the Task Force.

With an Expanded Definition, OMB's Inventory of Federal Data Centers Has Grown

OMB has used two different definitions for a data center throughout the life of FDCCI. In 2010, OMB defined a "data center" as any room used for the purpose of processing or storing data that is larger than 500 square feet, is used for processing or storing data, and meets stringent availability requirements.[9] While agencies included other facilities classified as a "server room" (typically smaller than 500 square feet) and "server closet" (typically smaller than 200 square feet) in their inventories, these facilities were not included in OMB's final tally of data centers. However, in October 2011, the Federal CIO expanded the definition to include a facility of any size. OMB further clarified its definition in March 2012, as follows:

"...a data center is...a closet, room, floor or building for the storage, management, and dissemination of data and information and [used to house] computer systems and associated components, such as database, application, and storage systems and data stores [excluding facilities exclusively devoted to communications and network equipment (e.g., telephone exchanges and telecommunications rooms)]. A data center generally includes redundant or backup power supplies, redundant data communications connections, environmental controls...and special security devices housed in leased, owned, collocated, or stand-alone facilities."[10]

Under the first definition, OMB identified 2,094 data centers in July 2010. Using the new definition from October 2011, OMB estimated that there were a total of 3,133 federal data centers in December 2011, and its goal was to consolidate approximately 40 percent, or 1,253 data centers, for a savings of approximately $3 billion by the end of 2015.

---

[9]For more information on the classifications used to define availability requirements, see Uptime Institute, *Industry Standard Tier Classifications Define Site Infrastructure Performance* (Santa Fe, N.Mex.: 2005).

[10]OMB, *Implementation Guidance for the Federal Data Center Consolidation Initiative* (Washington, D.C.: Mar. 19, 2012).

GAO-14-713 Data Center Consolidation

Since 2011, the number of federal data centers reported by agencies has continued to grow. In July 2013, we testified[11] that 22 of the 24 FDCCI agencies had collectively reported 6,836 data centers in their inventories—an increase of about 3,700 compared to OMB's previous estimate from December 2011. According to the Federal CIO, the increase in data centers was primarily due to the expanded definition of a data center and improved inventory reporting by the agencies.

More recently, our analysis of agencies' May 2014 data center inventories indicated that agencies collectively reported a total of 9,658 data centers. Of the total reported data centers, 242 were reported by agencies as "core" data centers—meaning that they are primary consolidation points for agency enterprise IT services and not planned for closure, while the remaining 9,416 were reported as "non-core."[12] OMB's March 2013 memorandum states that the goal is for agencies to close 40 percent of the total non-core data centers, or 3,766 data centers based on the May 2014 inventory data, by the end of fiscal year 2015.

Since 2011, agencies have reported their data center closures and planned closures on http://data.gov. As of May 2014, agencies collectively reported that they had closed a total of 976 data centers, and were planning to close an additional 2,689 data centers—for a total of 3,655—by the end of September 2015. See figure 1 for a summary of the total number of the federal data centers reported in agencies' inventories and closures as reported by agencies on http://data.gov over time, and table 1 for a depiction of the total number of data centers (including a breakdown of core and non-core centers) reported in agencies' May 2014 inventory submissions, and reported and planned closures.

---

[11]GAO-13-796T.

[12]According to OMB, as of July 2014, the total number of data centers collectively reported by agencies was 9,540, of which 275 were reported as core data centers and 9,265 were reported as non-core centers. OMB's tally of data centers differs from the number of data centers we found because, as we have previously reported, the number of data centers changes regularly as agencies update their inventories.

Figure 1: Total Number of Reported Federal Data Centers and Closures, as of May 2014

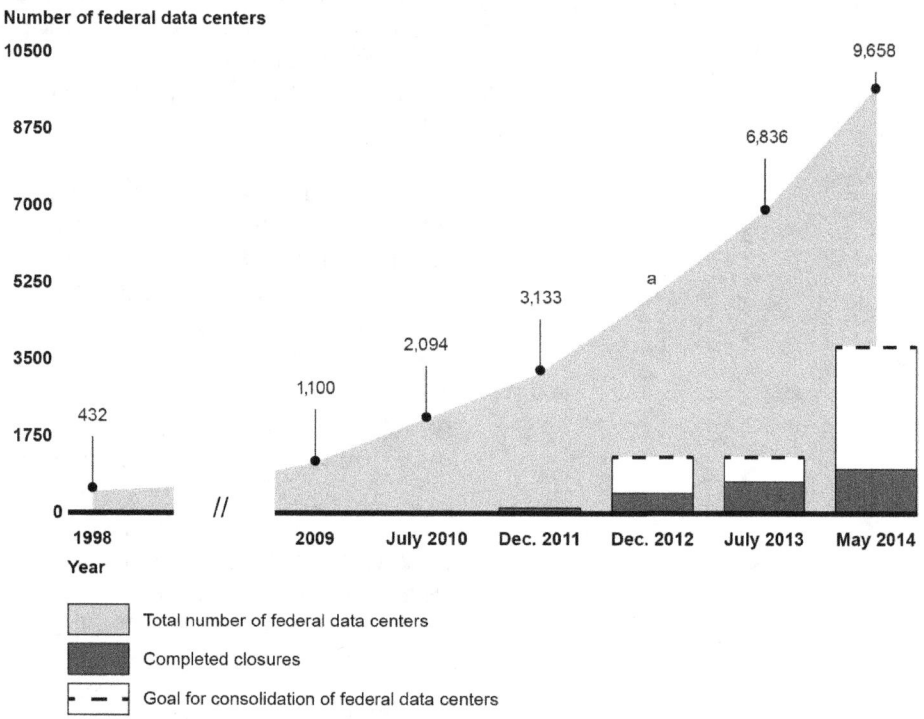

Number of federal data centers

Source: GAO analysis of OMB and agency data. | GAO-14-713

[a]OMB did not publically report the total number of data centers in 2012. OMB also expanded its definition of a data center in March 2012.

Table 1: Total Number of Core and Non-core Data Centers and Completed and Planned Closures by Agency, as of May 2014

Agency	Core data centers	Non-core data centers	Total number of data centers	Closures through May 2014 (percent of non-core centers closed)	Total planned for closure (percent of non-core centers closed)[a]
Agriculture	4	2,273	2,277	41 (2%)	2,254 (99%)
Commerce	32	327	359	66 (20%)	79 (24%)
Defense	11	2,297	2,308	374 (16%)	939 (41%)
Education	3	2	5	0 (0%)	2 (100%)
Energy	5	52	57	7 (13%)	19 (37%)
HHS	27	199	226	52 (26%)	67 (34%)
DHS	3	102	105	26 (25%)	56 (55%)
HUD	1	1	2	0 (0%)	0 (0%)
Interior	6	410	416	71 (17%)	133 (32%)
Justice	3	107	110	53 (50%)	66 (62%)
Labor	9	84	93	8 (10%)	17 (20%)
State	4	386	390	5 (1%)	9 (2%)
Transportation	16	517	533	42 (8%)	171 (33%)
Treasury	4	2,133	2,137	102 (5%)	111 (5%)
VA	87	257	344	15 (6%)	23 (9%)
EPA	4	77	81	19 (25%)	29 (38%)
GSA	4	119	123	60 (50%)	74 (62%)
NASA	11	48	59	25 (52%)	38 (79%)
NSF	0	2	2	1 (50%)	1 (50%)
NRC	1	8	9	0 (0%)	3 (38%)
OPM	4	0	4	0 (0%)	0 (0%)
SBA	0	4	4	0 (0%	2 (50%)
SSA	2	0	2	0 (0%)	0 (0%)
USAID	1	11	12	2 (18%)	3 (27%)
Totals	**242**	**9,416**	**9,658**	**969 (10%)**	**4,096 (44%)**

Source: GAO analysis of agency data. | GAO-14-713

Note: HHS—Department of Health and Human Services; DHS—Department of Homeland Security; HUD—Department of Housing and Urban Development; VA—Department of Veterans Affairs; EPA—Environmental Protection Agency; GSA—General Services Administration; NASA—National Aeronautics and Space Administration; NSF—National Science Foundation; NRC—Nuclear Regulatory Commission; OPM—Office of Personnel Management; SBA—Small Business Administration; SSA—Social Security Administration; USAID—U.S. Agency for International Development.

[a]Totals include data centers planned for closure beyond fiscal year 2015.

OMB Integrated FDCCI with Its PortfolioStat Initiative

In March 2012, OMB launched the PortfolioStat initiative, which requires agencies to conduct an annual agency-wide IT portfolio review to, among other things, reduce commodity IT[13] spending and demonstrate how its IT investments align with the agency's mission and business functions.[14] PortfolioStat is designed to assist agencies in assessing the current maturity of their IT portfolio management process, make decisions on eliminating duplication, and move to shared solutions in order to maximize the return on IT investments across the portfolio.

In September 2012, the Federal CIO wrote in an e-mail to agencies that OMB was planning to integrate FDCCI with the PortfolioStat initiative to allow agencies to focus on an enterprise-wide approach to address all commodity IT, including data centers, in an integrated, comprehensive plan and that agencies should continue to focus on optimizing those data centers that are essential to delivering taxpayer services, while continuing to close those that are duplicative. In addition, the e-mail directed agencies to delay submitting their October 1, 2012 submissions of updated consolidation plans until further guidance could be provided. However, agencies were still to report quarterly updates on their data center closures.

In March 2013, OMB issued a memorandum documenting the integration of FDCCI with PortfolioStat.[15] Among other things, the memorandum discussed OMB's efforts to further the PortfolioStat initiative by incorporating several changes, such as consolidating previously collected IT-related plans, reports, and data submissions. The guidance also stated that, to more effectively measure the efficiency of an agency's data center assets, agencies would also be measured by the extent to which their data centers are optimized for total cost of ownership by incorporating metrics for data center energy, facility, labor, and storage, among other things. OMB indicated in its memorandum that these metrics would be developed by the Task Force.

---

[13]According to OMB, commodity IT includes services such as IT infrastructure (data centers, networks, desktop computers and mobile devices); enterprise IT systems (e-mail, collaboration tools, identity and access management, security, and web infrastructure); and business systems (finance, human resources, and other administrative functions).

[14]OMB, *Implementing PortfolioStat*, Memorandum M-12-10 (Washington D.C.: Mar. 30, 2012).

[15]OMB, Memorandum M-13-09.

GAO-14-713 Data Center Consolidation

This March 2013 memorandum also established new agency reporting requirements and related time frames. Specifically, agencies were no longer required to submit the data center consolidation plans previously required under FDCCI. Rather, agencies were to submit information to OMB via three primary means—an information resources management strategic plan,[16] an enterprise road map,[17] and an integrated data collection channel.[18] In addition, agencies were still required to update their data center inventories yearly and report quarterly on http://data.gov regarding their consolidation progress.

More recently, in May 2014, OMB issued a memorandum updating its PortfolioStat guidance for fiscal year 2014.[19] As in past PortfolioStat guidance, the memorandum discussed the importance of PortfolioStat sessions—data-driven reviews of agency portfolio management between the Federal CIO, Agency Deputy Secretary, and other senior agency officials—as a means to continue to drive cost savings. OMB's guidance also reinforced the need for agencies to continue to consolidate their non-core data centers while optimizing their core data centers using metrics established by the Task Force, and documented in OMB's memorandum. These metrics are discussed in more detail later in this report.

---

[16]OMB, *Management of Federal Information Resources*, Circular A-130 (Washington, D.C.: Nov. 30, 2000). According to OMB Circular A-130, an agency's information resources management strategic plan should describe how information resources management activities help accomplish agency missions, and ensure that information resource management decisions are integrated with organizational planning, budget, procurement, financial management, human resources management, and program decisions.

[17]OMB, *Increasing Shared Approaches to Information Technology Services* (Washington, D.C.: May 2, 2012). The enterprise road map is to include a business and technology architecture, an IT asset inventory, a commodity IT consolidation plan, a line of business service plan, and an IT shared service plan.

[18]According to OMB, the integrated data collection channel is to be used by agencies to report structured information, such as progress in meeting IT strategic goals, objectives, and metrics, as well as cost savings and avoidances resulting from IT management actions.

[19]OMB, *Fiscal Year 2014 PortfolioStat*, Memorandum M-14-08 (Washington, D.C.: May 7, 2014).

GAO Has Reported and Testified on Issues Related to Consolidating Data Centers

We have previously reported on OMB's efforts to consolidate federal data centers. In March 2011, we identified data center consolidation as one of the 81 areas within the federal government with opportunities to reduce potential duplication, overlap, and fragmentation. In this regard, we reported on the status of FDCCI and noted that data center consolidation made sense economically and was a way to achieve more efficient IT operations, but that challenges existed.[20] For example, agencies reported facing challenges in ensuring the accuracy of their inventories and plans, providing upfront funding for the consolidation effort before any cost savings accrue, and overcoming cultural resistance to such major organizational changes, among other things.

In July 2011, we issued a report on the status of FDCCI and found that only 1 of the 24 agencies had submitted a complete inventory and no agency had submitted complete plans.[21] Further, OMB had not required agencies to document the steps they had taken, if any, to verify the inventory data. We concluded that until these inventories and plans were complete, agencies would not be able to implement their consolidation activities and realize expected cost savings. Moreover, without an understanding of the validity of agencies' consolidation data, OMB could not be assured that agencies were providing a sound baseline for estimating consolidation savings and measuring progress against those goals. Accordingly, we made several recommendations to OMB, including that the Federal CIO require that agencies, when updating their data center inventory, state what actions were taken to verify the information in the inventory and to identify any associated limitations on the data, and to complete the missing elements in their inventories and consolidation plans.

OMB generally agreed with our report and has since taken actions to address our recommendations. For example, in July 2011, OMB required agency CIOs to submit a letter that identified steps taken to verify their data center inventory information and attest to the completeness of their consolidation plan. In addition, in March 2012, OMB required that all agencies complete all elements missing from their consolidation plans by the end of the fourth quarter of every fiscal year.

---

[20]GAO, *Opportunities to Reduce Potential Duplication in Government Programs, Save Tax Dollars, and Enhance Revenue*, GAO-11-318SP (Washington, D.C.: Mar. 1, 2011).

[21]GAO-11-565.

Additionally, in July 2012, we updated our review of FDCCI's status and found that, while agencies' 2011 inventories and plans had improved as compared to their 2010 submissions, only 3 agencies had submitted a complete inventory and only 1 agency had submitted a complete consolidation plan.[22] In addition, we noted that 3 agencies had submitted their inventory using an outdated format, in part, because OMB had not publicly posted its revised guidance. Notwithstanding these weaknesses, we noted that 19 agencies reported anticipating about $2.4 billion in cost savings between 2011 and 2015.

We also reported that none of five selected agencies had a master program schedule or cost-benefit analysis that was fully consistent with best practices. To assist agencies with their data center consolidation efforts, OMB had sponsored the development of a FDCCI total cost of ownership[23] model that was intended to help agencies refine their estimated costs for consolidation; however, agencies were not required to use the cost model as part of their cost estimating efforts. Accordingly, we reiterated our prior recommendation that agencies complete missing plan and inventory elements and made new recommendations to OMB to publically post guidance updates on the FDCCI website and to require agencies to use its cost model.

OMB generally agreed with our recommendations and has since taken steps to address them. More specifically, OMB posted its 2012 guidance for updating data center inventories and plans, as well as guidance for reporting consolidation progress, to the FDCCI public website. Further, the website has been updated to provide prior guidance documents and OMB memorandums. In addition, OMB's 2012 consolidation plan guidance required agencies to use the cost model as they developed their 2014 budget request.

More recently, in April 2013, we reported[24] on OMB and agencies' progress in consolidating federal data centers. Specifically, we reported that the 24 agencies participating in FDCCI had made progress by closing a total of 420 data centers by the end of December 2012. However, OMB

---

[22]GAO-12-742.

[23]OMB refers to total cost of ownership as all associated data center-related activities and costs without regard to ownership, project association, or funding line.

[24]GAO-13-378.

had not measured agencies' progress against key performance measures, including its cost savings goal, or ensured that other key oversight responsibilities, such as approving agencies consolidation plans on the basis of their completeness, were being fully executed. We reported that OMB had not determined agencies' progress against its cost savings goal because, according to OMB staff, the agency had not determined a consistent and repeatable method for tracking cost savings and that the weaknesses in oversight were due, in part, to OMB not ensuring that assigned responsibilities were being executed. Accordingly, we recommended that OMB track and report on key performance measures, including cost savings, and improve the execution of important oversight responsibilities. OMB generally agreed with our recommendations and has since taken some initial actions to implement them, including tracking and reporting on data center consolidation cost savings on a quarterly basis.

Finally, between May 2013 and June 2014, we testified[25] on the status of FDCCI. Notably, in July 2013, we testified that, while agencies continued to make progress by closing an additional 64 data centers compared to the total number reported through the end of December 2012, the number of federal data centers had grown significantly since OMB's December 2011 estimate of approximately 3,133 data centers. Specifically, 22 of the 24 FDCCI agencies had collectively reported 6,836 data centers in their inventories—an increase of about 3,700 as compared to OMB's previous estimate from December 2011.[26] We concluded that it would be important for OMB to be transparent on agencies' progress against its performance metrics going forward.

---

[25]GAO-14-671T, GAO-14-596T, GAO-13-796T, GAO-13-685T, and GAO-13-627T.

[26]As previously mentioned, as of May 2014, agencies had collectively reported a total of 9,658 data centers—an increase of 2,822 compared to what agencies had reported as of July 2013.

Agencies Have Planned Substantial Consolidation Savings, but Reporting Can Be Improved

For FDCCI, OMB originally established a goal of achieving $3 billion in cost savings by the end of 2015. Pursuant to this goal, agencies have reported achieving more than a billion dollars in savings and avoidances through fiscal year 2013 and are planning a total of about $3.3 billion in savings and avoidances by the end of fiscal year 2015—an amount that is approximately $300 million higher than OMB's goal. Between fiscal years 2011 and 2017, agencies reported planning approximately $5.3 billion in total savings and avoidances. However, planned cost savings may be higher because six agencies with as many as 67 data center closures each have been limited in their abilities to fully report their savings. In addition, slightly more than half of agencies with planned cost savings are underreporting their fiscal years 2012 through 2015 figures to OMB by approximately $2.2 billion. While several agencies noted internal agency communication issues as the reasons for not reporting savings to OMB, other agencies were unable to provide a reason. Until agencies fully report their savings, the total planned cost savings and avoidances of $5.3 billion will be understated.

Agencies' Reported Savings Exceed More than a Billion Dollars through Fiscal Year 2013; Significant Additional Savings Planned through Fiscal Year 2017

Since launching FDCCI in 2010, achieving cost savings has been a primary goal of the initiative. As previously discussed, one of the original high-level objectives was to reduce the costs of data center hardware, software, and operations. OMB subsequently expanded on this goal and, in February 2012, stated that data center consolidation had the potential to achieve $3 billion dollars in savings by the end of 2015. Pursuant to these goals, OMB required agencies to describe year-by-year investments and cost savings in their 2010 and 2011 consolidation plans and, beginning in August 2013, has required agencies to identify and report all cost savings and avoidances[27] related to data center consolidation, among other areas, to OMB as part of a quarterly data collection process known as the integrated data collection.[28]

---

[27]OMB budget guidance defines cost savings as a reduction in actual expenditures below the projected level of costs to achieve a specific objective and defines cost avoidances as results from an action taken in the immediate time frame that will decrease costs in the future.

[28]OMB, Memorandum M-13-09. According to OMB's guidance, the integrated data collection is to be used by agencies to report structured information, such as progress in meeting IT strategic goals, objectives, and metrics, as well as cost savings and avoidances resulting from IT management actions, including data center consolidation.

Most of the 24 agencies are achieving cost savings or avoidances from their data center consolidation efforts. Specifically, between fiscal years 2011 and 2013, 19 agencies collectively reported achieving an estimated $1.1 billion in cost savings and avoidances. Notably, Defense, the Department of Homeland Security (DHS), and the Department of the Treasury (Treasury) account for approximately $850 million (or 74 percent) of the reported estimated savings through fiscal year 2013. The remaining 5 agencies that did not report savings between fiscal years 2011 and 2013 cited varied reasons for not being able to do so, which included difficulties in determining baseline data center costs, upfront costs that have exceeded savings to date, and a lack of electrical metering to determine power usage savings.

The methodologies used to calculate savings varied across the 19 agencies that reported estimated or actual savings and avoidances through fiscal year 2013; however, most of these agencies estimated their figures. Specifically, 3 agencies—the Department of Education (Education), EPA, and the National Science Foundation (NSF)—reported actual cost savings and avoidances, which they determined by calculating differences in executed budget or contract amounts over time. The remaining 16 agencies estimated their cost savings and avoidances. As examples, GSA estimated its savings using the department's total cost of ownership model; the Department of the Interior (Interior) used post-consolidation forms collected from its component bureaus and offices to estimate cost savings related to areas such as rent, utilities, and personnel after a consolidation activity was completed; and Treasury estimated savings resulting from reductions in the percentage of IT infrastructure investment spending as compared to total IT spending over time. Officials at these agencies stated that they were limited to reporting estimating savings because of challenges in determining actual savings, including the lack of electrical metering to calculate power usage savings, budget and accounting systems that are not structured to account for the costs of individual data centers, and difficulties in determining costs and savings when data centers are located in multipurpose facilities. These issues are discussed in more detail later in this report.

See table 2 for a listing of agencies' data center closures, cost savings and cost avoidances between fiscal years 2011 and 2013, and whether the agency savings are estimated.

Table 2: Agency-reported Data Center Consolidation Cost Savings and Avoidances (FY 2011 through FY 2013)

Dollars in millions (rounded)

Agency	Data center closures reported on data.gov, as of May 2014	FY 2011 actual or estimated savings and avoidances	FY 2012 actual or estimated savings and avoidances	FY 2013 actual or estimated savings and avoidances	Total cost savings and avoidances[a]	Estimated or actual cost savings and avoidances
Agriculture	41	$0	$27.63	$43.67	$71.30	Estimated
Commerce	68	6.15	17.04	29.58	52.77	Estimated
Defense	374	11.57	19.16	104.84	135.57	Estimated
Education	0	0	.25	.24	.49	Actual
Energy	7	1.80	.20	1.18	3.18	Estimated
HHS	52	0	0	4.34	4.34	Estimated
DHS	26	0	43.19	93.11	136.30	Estimated
HUD	0	0	0	0	0	None reported
Interior	65	.12	3.76	8.96	12.84	Estimated
Justice	54	.29	2.26	3.73	6.28	Estimated
Labor	11	0	0	0	0	None reported
State	5	1.60	3.53	5.68	10.81	Estimated
Transportation	42	0	10.06	21.25	31.31	Estimated
Treasury[b]	102	170.23	112.19	295.24	577.66	Estimated
VA	15	0	5.17	6.37	11.54	Estimated
EPA[b]	19	.37	17.88	52.55	70.80	Actual
GSA	67	0	3.38	9.47	12.85	Estimated
NASA	25	.17	.47	.66	1.30	Estimated
NSF	1	0	1.18	2.50	3.68	Actual
NRC	0	0	.09	0	.09	Estimated
OPM	0	0	.32	0	.32	Estimated
SBA	0	0	0	0	0	None reported
SSA	0	0	0	0	0	None reported
USAID	2	0	0	0	0	None reported
Totals	**976**	**192.30**	**267.76**	**683.37**	**1,143.43**	

Key: FY = fiscal year.

Source: GAO analysis of agency and OMB data. | GAO-14-713

Note: HHS—Department of Health and Human Services; DHS—Department of Homeland Security; HUD—Department of Housing and Urban Development; VA—Department of Veterans Affairs; EPA—Environmental Protection Agency; GSA—General Services Administration; NASA—National Aeronautics and Space Administration; NSF—National Science Foundation; NRC—Nuclear Regulatory Commission; OPM—Office of Personnel Management; SBA—Small Business Administration; SSA—Social Security Administration; USAID—U.S. Agency for International Development.

ᵇFor noted agencies, data center consolidation savings and avoidances were reported in the context of their broader IT infrastructure modernization efforts because of difficulties in separating out data center consolidation-specific savings.

As prescribed by OMB's initial guidance on data center consolidation, the 19 agencies that reported achieving cost savings and avoidances did so using a variety of approaches. While these approaches can be grouped into four key areas—decommissioning, consolidation, cloud computing, and virtualization—agencies generally employed, and achieved cost savings and avoidances using, multiple approaches at the same time. For example, NSF officials stated that in order to reduce the agency's dependence on onsite infrastructure, the agency has been focused on increasing virtualization and consolidation of servers and storage, while continuing to adopt cloud computing technologies. See table 3 for a description of the four approaches and key examples of agency-reported savings or avoidances in each.

Table 3: Consolidation Approaches and Key Examples of Agency-reported Cost Savings and Avoidances

Approach	Selected agencies and key examples of reported cost savings and avoidances
Decommissioning Reducing underutilized or redundant physical servers or entire data centers. Examples include moving to an outsourced data center or reducing the number of physical assets.	• **DHS** – $136.30 million in cost savings between FY 2012 and FY 2013 due primarily to the decommissioning of component agency physical servers and operations and migrating to DHS's enterprise data centers. • **Defense** – $67.07 million in estimated savings between FY 2011 and FY 2013 due to facility closures resulting in eliminating staff and reducing the facility costs per square foot. • **VA** – $11.54 million in cost avoidances between FY 2012 and FY 2013 due to migrating portions of its Veterans Health Information System and Technology Architecture to the Defense Information System Agency's enterprise computing centers, versus utilizing commercially leased data centers.
Consolidation Combining workload onto fewer computers or concentrating data processing into fewer physical facilities can help to reduce the cost of data center hardware, software, and operations, in addition to real estate and energy costs.	• **Treasury** – $577.66 million in estimated avoidances between FY 2011 and FY 2013 due to reductions in the percentage of IT infrastructure spending compared to total IT spending due to consolidation efforts within its end-user, network, and server investments. • **Agriculture** – $71.30 million in estimated savings and avoidances between FY 2012 and FY2013 from reduced hardware and software maintenance and support costs; hardware refresh costs; data center energy and operational costs; and personnel costs from its consolidation effort. • **EPA** – $10.00 million in cost savings in FY 2012 due to a reduction in shared services costs (e.g., e-mail and licenses) as a result of the agency's IT infrastructure consolidation and optimization efforts.

Approach	Selected agencies and key examples of reported cost savings and avoidances
Cloud computing Cloud computing relies on Internet-based services and resources to provide computing services to customers. Examples include web-based e-mail applications and common business applications that are accessed online instead of through a local computer.	• **Commerce** – $18.30 million in estimated cost avoidances between FY 2011 through FY 2013 at the Census Bureau as a result of its private cloud initiative. • **Education** – $.49 million in cost savings and avoidances between FY 2012 and FY 2013 due to reduced power consumption as a result of moving servers and other IT services to contractor-owned and operated facilities using a cloud-based infrastructure. • **OPM** – $.32 million in estimated savings in FY 2012 by moving systems and servers to a combination of private and public cloud solutions.
Virtualization Virtualization is a technology that allows multiple software-based virtual machines that have different operating systems, to run in isolation, side by side, on the same physical machine. Virtualization is often used as part of cloud computing.	• **Defense** – $68.51 million in estimated savings in FY 2013 from efficiencies achieved, in part, through virtualization and operating system reductions, among other related areas. • **State** – $9.21 million in estimated cost avoidances between FY 2012 and FY 2013 due to the agency's virtualization effort, which enabled it to avoid costs associated with maintaining physical servers (e.g., hardware, power, and cooling). • **NSF** – $1.18 million in cost avoidances in FY 2012 due to the agency's server virtualization effort, which avoided costs related to maintenance and replacement of more than 100 legacy servers.

Key: FY = fiscal year.

Source: GAO analysis of agency data. | GAO-14-713

Note: DHS—Department of Homeland Security; VA—Department of Veterans Affairs; EPA—Environmental Protection Agency; OPM—Office of Personnel Management; NSF—National Science Foundation.

In addition to savings through fiscal year 2013, our analysis of estimated future savings shows that, collectively, agencies are reporting that they expect to exceed OMB's cost savings goal by the end of fiscal year 2015 and continue to achieve significant savings in future years. Specifically, 21 agencies collectively reported planning a total of about $3.3 billion in savings and avoidances by the end of 2015—an amount that is approximately $300 million higher than OMB's original $3 billion goal. Further, through fiscal year 2017, these agencies collectively reported planning an additional $2.1 billion in cost savings and avoidances, for a total of approximately $5.3 billion. Five agencies—the Department of Agriculture (Agriculture), Defense, DHS, the Department of Transportation (Transportation), and Treasury—account for about $4.9 billion (or approximately 91 percent) of the total savings reported. See table 4 for a listing of agencies' total cost savings and cost avoidances between fiscal years 2011 and 2017.

Table 4: Agency-reported Total Data Center Consolidation Cost Savings and Avoidances (FY 2011 through FY 2017)

Dollars in millions (rounded)

Agency	FY 2011 through FY 2013 actual and estimated cost savings and avoidances	Planned cost savings and avoidances estimated by agencies				
		FY 2014	FY 2015	FY 2016	FY 2017	Totals[a,b]
Agriculture	$71.30	$71.14	$101.73	n.d.	n.d.	$244.17
Commerce	52.77	22.25	8.09	1.98	1.49	86.58
Defense[c]	135.57	144.75	415.75	801.56	1,120.69	2,618.32
Education	.49	.24	.24	.24	n.d.	1.21
Energy	3.18	.57	.57	11.75	8.59	24.66
HHS	4.34	8.97	12.11	n.d.	n.d.	25.42
DHS	136.30	53.58	4.70	4.86	6.49	205.93
HUD	0	n.d.	n.d.	n.d.	n.d.	0
Interior	12.84	27.27	44.43	n.d.	n.d.	84.54
Justice	6.28	3.86	n.d.	n.d.	n.d.	10.14
Labor	0	.39	.85	n.d.	n.d.	1.24
State	10.81	7.63	11.60	0	0	30.04
Transportation	31.31	42.80	66.07	88.95	n.d.	229.13
Treasury	577.66	469.65	528.60	n.d.	n.d.	1,575.91
VA	11.54	6.37	6.37	6.37	6.37	37.02
EPA	70.80	.50	.65	.65	n.d.	72.60
GSA	12.85	15.30	20.65	n.d.	n.d.	48.80
NASA	1.30	.66	.66	.66	n.d.	3.28
NSF	3.68	3.07	.06	n.d.	n.d.	6.81
NRC	.09	n.d.	n.d.	n.d.	n.d.	.09
OPM	.32	3.08	n.d.	n.d.	n.d.	3.40
SBA	0	0	0	0	0	0
SSA	0	13.30	27.05	n.d.	n.d.	40.35
USAID	0	0	0	0	n.d.	0
Total	**1,143.43**	**895.38**	**1,250.18**	**917.02**	**1,143.63**	**5,349.64**

Key: FY = fiscal year; n.d. = no data.

Source: GAO analysis of agency data. | GAO-14-713

Note: HHS—Department of Health and Human Services; DHS—Department of Homeland Security; HUD—Department of Housing and Urban Development; VA—Department of Veterans Affairs; EPA—Environmental Protection Agency; GSA—General Services Administration; NASA—National Aeronautics and Space Administration; NSF—National Science Foundation; NRC—Nuclear Regulatory Commission; OPM—Office of Personnel Management; SBA—Small Business Administration; SSA—Social Security Administration; USAID—U.S. Agency for International Development.

[a]These figures do not fully reflect the costs associated with agencies' data center consolidation efforts because many agencies faced challenges in determining these costs, as discussed later in this report.

GAO-14-713 Data Center Consolidation

bThree agencies—DHS, Energy, and VA—reported a total of approximately $62.07 million in additional savings between fiscal years 2018 and 2021; however, these savings are not reflected in the table because the remaining 21 agencies did not have data for these fiscal years.

cAccording to Defense officials, the department's planned cost savings figures are expected to vary over time as more data center assets are discovered, component agency plans mature, and estimating techniques continue to improve.

The extent of cost savings and avoidances being reported by agencies beyond fiscal year 2015 highlights the importance of OMB continuing to track and report on such savings beyond the time frame of its initial goal. Further, with many agencies having not yet reported on their planned savings, the savings beyond fiscal year 2015 may be higher than previously discussed. In this regard, we have previously recommended that OMB extend the horizon for realizing cost savings from FDCCI, as doing so could provide OMB and FDCCI stakeholders with input and information on the benefits of consolidation beyond OMB's initial goal.[29] OMB neither agreed nor disagreed with our recommendation but stated that, as the FDCCI and PortfolioStat initiatives proceed and continue to generate savings, OMB would consider whether updates to the current time frame are appropriate.

Savings May Be Higher than Current Amounts Due to Underreporting of Planned Savings by Many Agencies

As previously mentioned, OMB's March 2013 memorandum[30] identified the requirements for reporting cost savings from data center consolidation. Specifically, the memorandum stated that agencies are required to report their data center consolidation cost savings and avoidances, among other areas, to OMB as part of a quarterly integrated data collection process. OMB's May 2014 memorandum[31] reiterated the requirements for integrated data collection submissions. Agencies can currently input cost savings and avoidances for fiscal years 2012 through 2015 into the web-based portal used to submit their integrated data collection submissions. Finally, standards for internal control emphasize the need for federal agencies to establish plans to help ensure goals and

---

[29]GAO-13-378.

[30]OMB, Memorandum M-13-09.

[31]OMB, Memorandum M-14-08.

objectives can be met, including compliance with applicable laws and regulations.[32]

Although agencies are already collectively reporting approximately $5.3 billion in planned cost savings and avoidances from their consolidation efforts, these savings may be higher because 6 of the 24 agencies, claiming between 11 and 67 data center closures each, have been limited in their abilities to report savings. For example, although Interior reported closing 65 data centers as of May 2014, the agency cited significant challenges in obtaining costs and related savings information from its component agencies. In addition, the National Aeronautics and Space Administration (NASA) reported that, as of May 2014, it had closed 25 data centers; however, while the agency has been able to report $1.3 million in savings through fiscal year 2013, agency officials stated that NASA has been otherwise limited in its ability to identify cost savings and avoidances because of the agency's complex organizational structure, which includes multiple centers with multiple missions and multiple IT contractors utilizing data centers within multipurpose facilities. Similar challenges were also identified by other agencies, as discussed later in this report. Table 5 shows the agencies with limited or no savings relative to their consolidation efforts and their reasons for not being able to fully report savings.

[32]GAO, *Standards for Internal Control in the Federal Government,* GAO-14-704G (Washington, D.C.: Sept. 10, 2014).

Table 5: Agencies with Substantial Consolidation Efforts but Limited or No Savings Reported

Dollars in millions (rounded)

Agency	Data center closures reported on data.gov, as of May 2014	Agency-reported estimated savings (FY 2011 through FY 2013)	Reason(s) for limited or no savings or avoidances reported
HHS	52	$4.34	HHS officials stated that significant savings have likely been realized from the closure of the agency's data centers, but the agency lacks the data needed to identify and document cost savings. Officials added that the CIO is developing a plan that is expected to address the challenges associated with the identification and documentation of cost savings; however, no time frame for completion of this plan has been established.
Interior	65	12.84	While Interior has developed a process to collect cost savings information from its components, officials stated that individual bureaus and offices often do not have the detailed information to report on data center-specific savings because they do not have complete information about their facility costs (including power usage) and therefore cannot determine the facility cost savings.
Justice	54	6.28	Justice officials stated that that the department's decentralized organizational structure and culture have made it challenging to implement the data center consolidation initiative, but that more detailed plans to more aggressively consolidate and optimize IT services are being developed as the department collaboratively explores opportunities with its component agencies. However, no time frame has been established for completion of these plans.
Labor	11	0	Labor officials stated that the department's primary challenge in determining and measuring cost savings stems from issues in developing a baseline of the costs of IT services from which to calculate savings, but also noted that there is a lag between the time data centers are closed and when cost reductions can be realized. Officials added that consolidating and relocating systems and data centers to the department's enterprise data center is expected to provide the department with the capability to better measure data center costs; however, officials were unsure when the department would be able to determine cost savings.
GSA	67	12.85	GSA officials stated that, while the agency has had success in improving the quality of its data center inventory, it has been challenged in determining data center-specific costs, cost savings, and cost avoidances. Officials stated that this is partly due to its decentralized organizational structure where data center costs (e.g., rents, leases, personnel, equipment repair, and replacement and service contracts) are distributed across 11 regions and six component agencies and their subordinate organizations.
NASA	25	1.30	NASA officials stated that the agency has been unable to capture actual cost savings and avoidances for its data center consolidation effort because of various challenges, including the agency's complex organizational structure which includes multiple centers with multiple missions and multiple IT contractors utilizing data centers within multipurpose facilities—all of which make determining savings extremely complex and impractical. Officials noted that the agency has focused primarily on closing data centers and improving server densities at the agency's core data centers.

Key: FY = fiscal year.

Source: GAO analysis of agency data and interviews, and OMB data. | GAO-14-713

Note: HHS—Department of Health and Human Services; GSA—General Services Administration; NASA—National Aeronautics and Space Administration.

Considering that cost savings is one of OMB's original high-level goals of FDCCI and reporting such savings is currently required on a quarterly basis, OMB has a responsibility for ensuring that agencies are identifying the full extent of cost savings from their consolidation efforts. Further, as previously mentioned, OMB's PortfolioStat guidance requires yearly review sessions of agency portfolio management (including data center consolidation) with the Federal CIO and senior agency officials and notes that these reviews are critical to driving cost savings.[33] We previously found[34] that all agencies held PortfolioStat sessions with OMB in fiscal year 2012. In addition, agencies were required to hold sessions again in 2013.[35] However, after 2 years of PortfolioStat sessions, the six agencies identified in the table have been limited in their ability to report savings from their data center consolidation efforts.

In addition, slightly more than half of the agencies with cost savings and avoidances did not fully report them to OMB—a requirement of OMB's quarterly integrated data collection process. Specifically, of the 21 agencies with actual and estimated fiscal years 2012 through 2015 cost savings and avoidances, 10 agencies fully reported their savings and avoidances to OMB through the integrated data collection process, 8 agencies partially reported this information, and 3 agencies did not report it.[36] As a result, agencies collectively reported savings for fiscal years 2012 through 2015 of approximately $3.1 billion to us, as compared to only about $876 million that agencies reported to OMB, meaning that the savings have been underreported to OMB by approximately $2.2 billion. See table 6 for a listing of agencies and a comparison of their data center consolidation savings as reported to GAO and through OMB's integrated data collection process.

---

[33]OMB, Memorandum M-14-08.

[34]GAO, *Information Technology: Additional OMB and Agency Actions Are Needed to Achieve Portfolio Savings,* GAO-14-65 (Washington, D.C.: Nov. 6, 2013).

[35]We have ongoing work looking at the status of the required fiscal year 2013 PortfolioStat actions, including agencies holding PortfolioStat sessions.

[36]Three agencies—the Department of Housing and Urban Development, the Small Business Administration, and the U.S. Agency for International Development—did not have actual or estimated savings or avoidances between fiscal years 2012 and 2015.

Table 6: Comparison of Agency Consolidation Savings and Avoidances Reported to GAO against Agency Integrated Data Collection Submissions (as of May 2014)

Dollars in millions (rounded)

| Agency | Cost savings and avoidances (FY 2012 through FY 2015) | | |
	Reported to GAO	Reported to OMB via the integrated data collection process[a]	Were savings and avoidances reported to OMB?
Agriculture	$244.17	$71.20	Partially
Commerce	76.96	71.59	Partially
Defense	684.50	268.75	Partially
Education	.97	.97	Yes
Energy	2.52	1.19	Partially
HHS	25.42	28.66	Yes
DHS	194.58	194.58	Yes
HUD	0	0	N/A
Interior	84.42	13.59	Partially
Justice	9.85	9.85	Yes
Labor	1.24	1.24	Yes
State	28.44	28.44	Yes
Transportation	140.18	7.36	Partially
Treasury	1,405.68	12.01	Partially
VA	24.28	0	No
EPA	71.58	70.93	Partially
GSA	48.80	48.80	Yes
NASA	2.45	0	No
NSF	6.81	6.81	Yes
NRC	.09	.09	Yes
OPM	3.40	0	No
SBA	0	0	N/A
SSA	40.35	40.35	Yes
USAID	0	0	N/A
Total	**3,096.69**	**876.41**	

Key: FY = fiscal year; N/A = Not applicable. Agency did not report any cost savings or avoidances.

Source: GAO analysis of agency data. | GAO-14-713

Note: HHS—Department of Health and Human Services; DHS—Department of Homeland Security; HUD—Department of Housing and Urban Development; VA—Department of Veterans Affairs; EPA—Environmental Protection Agency; GSA—General Services Administration; NASA—National Aeronautics and Space Administration; NSF—National Science Foundation; NRC—Nuclear Regulatory Commission; OPM—Office of Personnel Management; SBA—Small Business Administration; SSA—Social Security Administration; USAID—U.S. Agency for International Development.

While several agencies noted internal agency communication issues as a reason that their savings and avoidances were not fully reported, other agencies were not able to provide a reason. These shortcomings in agency reporting have resulted in OMB not being able to fully report agencies' data center consolidation cost savings and avoidances in its quarterly reports to Congress on the status of federal IT reform efforts, in accordance with its responsibilities as set forth in law. For example, OMB's May 2014 report to Congress[37] noted total fiscal years 2012 and 2013 data center consolidation cost savings and avoidances of slightly less than $329 million, as compared to the approximately $951 million that agencies reported to us that they achieved over that same time period—a difference of approximately $622 million.

Until OMB assists those agencies with limited or no cost savings reported, agencies may not be able to identify the full extent of savings from their consolidation efforts and the total planned cost savings and avoidances of approximately $5.3 billion will be understated. Further, until agencies fully report their cost savings and avoidances to OMB, Congress may be limited in its ability to oversee agencies' progress against key initiative goals.

Agencies Reported Successes and Challenges in Achieving Cost Savings

Nearly all agencies reported experiencing differing types of success in achieving cost savings. Specifically, 22 of the 24 agencies identified a total of 21 types of success,[38] while the remaining 2 agencies—the Department of Housing and Urban Development (HUD) and the Small Business Administration (SBA)—did not identify any. Five types of successes were identified by five agencies or more, with the most-reported being identified by 22 agencies. Table 7 details the reported successes as well as the number of related agencies; the most common successes are further discussed after the table.

---

[37]OMB, *Quarterly Report to Congress: Information Technology Oversight and Reform* (Washington, D.C.: May 6, 2014).

[38]Agencies did not always have reportable cost savings or avoidances in areas noted as successes due, in part, to challenges in quantifying their savings and avoidances (as discussed throughout this report).

Table 7: Agency Consolidation Successes in Achieving Cost Savings

Successes	Number of agencies
Focused on virtualization and cloud services as consolidation solutions	22
Reduced power consumption	7
Reduced facility costs (e.g., rent and maintenance)	6
Ensured a more comprehensive asset inventory	6
Standardized IT capabilities (e.g., hardware, software, and security architecture)	5
Provided data center services (e.g., cloud infrastructure and hosting services) to other agencies to decrease costs or increase revenues	2
Realized savings and efficiencies from the migration to enterprise data centers	2
Used data centers owned, leased, or operated by other agencies	2
Eliminated duplicative investments in IT hardware, software and support services	2
More efficiently delivered computing services	2
Instituted a culture of continuous process improvement to seek new, cost effective methods, tools, and solutions for data center migration	1
Improved internal agency coordination between the CIO and Chief Financial Officer	1
Implemented cultural changes (e.g., teleworking) to facilitate consolidation	1
Identified additional opportunities for consolidation through a space management assessment	1
Renegotiated shared service labor contracts	1
Increased CIO budget authority	1
Used energy savings performance contracts	1
Worked with component agencies to find consolidation opportunities	1
Increased granularity of infrastructure investments (i.e., end user, network, and server investments) to increase transparency and better identify savings	1
Improved data center consolidation-related planning	1
Implemented lessons learned and consolidation best practices, such as developing tools for identifying network, server, and storage utilization statistics	1

Source: GAO analysis of agency data and interviews with agency officials. | GAO-14-713

Nearly All Agencies Reported That Virtualization and Cloud Services Have Produced Cost Savings

Twenty-two agencies reported that focusing on virtualization and cloud services have proven successful in achieving cost savings. Virtualization is a technology that allows multiple, software-based machines with different operating systems, to run in isolation, side by side, on the same physical machine. Cloud computing is a form of computing that relies on Internet-based services and resources to provide computing services to customers, while freeing them from the burden and costs of maintaining the underlying infrastructure. As previously mentioned, OMB suggests that agencies use a combination of approaches—two of which are virtualization and cloud computing—in their consolidation efforts. In 2012, we found that 9 agencies reported that focusing on virtualization and cloud computing had helped improve their consolidation efforts.[39]

As noted previously, Defense reported about $68.51 million in estimated savings in fiscal year 2013 from efficiencies achieved, in part, through virtualization and operating system reductions. Defense officials noted that the department's current goal is a 30 percent reduction in operating systems by the end of fiscal year 2017. In addition, the Department of State (State) reported $9.21 million in estimated cost avoidances between fiscal years 2012 and 2013 to OMB due to the department's virtualization effort, which enabled it to avoid costs associated with maintaining physical servers (e.g., hardware, power, and cooling).

As another example, NSF officials stated that virtualization had helped the agency reduce its server footprint by more than 100 servers in fiscal year 2012, resulting in related cost avoidances of $1.18 million. Officials noted that the reduction in servers reduced the labor required to support the servers, the funding needed for hardware maintenance renewals, and the costs to implement future hardware upgrades. Finally, in its quarterly report to OMB, Transportation stated that the department reduced one of its data center's floor space by 62 percent and the number of physical servers from 88 to 34 in fiscal year 2013 by leveraging virtualization solutions. According to the department, this led to reduced costs for operations and maintenance, as well as a number of other benefits, including enhanced security protection, scalability, and disaster recovery activities.

In addition, agencies also shared with us the advantages of moving their organizations to cloud services and the resulting cost savings. For example, EPA reported that it consolidated its e-mail services to its private cloud, reducing the number of e-mail servers from over 180 to 20 and standardizing its e-mail data and archive management practices.

---

[39]GAO-12-742.

According to the agency, this resulted in savings of $1 million in fiscal year 2012. Further, in its quarterly submission to OMB, GSA reported that it expects to save slightly more than $12 million over 4 years, when compared to the considered alternative, by switching its e-mail services to a cloud provider. Agriculture also reported that it uses cloud services to host most of its major applications, which resulted in increased server utilization and reduced operating costs, among other things. For example, the department reported that its cloud environments operated at average server utilization rates of 55 to 65 percent versus the 10 to 20 percent average utilization rates it typically found across its legacy server environments.

Many Agencies Reported Success in Reducing Data Center Power Consumption and Facility Costs to Achieve Savings

Seven agencies reported that reducing power consumption had proven successful in achieving cost savings. For example, NASA reported that its consolidation efforts at the Kennedy Space Center had eliminated 913 servers, which reduced power consumption by approximately three million kilowatt hours per year and resulted in estimated cost savings of $288,000 annually. In addition, Energy reported that it saved an estimated $130,000 annually due to reduced power consumption resulting from the consolidation of two of its data centers. Further, Education reported that by shutting down the air conditioning units in 25 local area network closets it was able to reduce power consumption and achieve savings of approximately $247,000 between fiscal years 2011 and 2012. The Department of Commerce (Commerce), Defense, NSF, and the Nuclear Regulatory Commission (NRC) also stated that reduced power consumption successfully resulted in cost savings.

Six agencies also reported that they had been successful in reducing their data center facility costs. For example, Defense reported that facility closures, with resulting reductions in staff and facility costs, had resulted in $67.07 million in estimated savings between fiscal years 2011 and 2013. Similarly, Energy reported that it avoided $7.3 million in facility costs related to operations and maintenance expenses by closing two data centers. Further, the Department of Health and Human Services (HHS) reported saving about $2.3 million from fiscal years 2011 to 2013 by reducing facility costs. This was due to rent and generator maintenance fees that no longer needed to be paid after a data center was closed in fiscal year 2011. Commerce reported almost $2 million in savings and avoidances related to reduced facility costs as a result of its consolidation effort. Finally, NASA reported that it was able to reduce facility costs through a reduction of slightly more than 28,000 square feet of floor space at its Kennedy Space Center, for estimated savings of about $247,000 annually.

Improved Asset Inventories Have Helped Agencies Better Achieve Savings

Six agencies reported that having a more comprehensive data center inventory led to cost savings. DHS officials stated that improved information in the department's data center inventory helped to better plan data center relocations. The department noted that, while this did not cut down on the cost of consolidation, it served to improve DHS's ability to project the actual costs of, and savings related to, data center migrations to its enterprise data centers. In addition, Defense officials stated that the department had been able to leverage authorities granted to the CIO in the National Defense Authorization Act for Fiscal Year 2012[40] to withhold funding from component organizations that do not submit accurate and up-to-date data center inventories on time to the CIO. Officials added that these authorities have significantly helped the department in its consolidation effort and in achieving cost savings. As another example, State reported that updates and changes to its data center inventory had resulted in a more complete and accurate picture of the department's data center environment. The department also reported using the updated totals for servers, floor space, and power consumption to calculate its cost avoidances. Commerce, NASA, and Transportation also reported benefits from an improved data center inventory.

Standardization of IT Services Improved Capability Delivery, Resulting in Cost Savings

Five agencies also reported success through the standardization of IT capabilities. For example, EPA reported that the agency had achieved $10 million in cost savings in fiscal year 2012 due to the standardization of IT services such as adopting agency-wide IT procurement, consolidating to an agency-wide help desk, optimizing its disaster recovery practices, and reducing software licenses through shared services. As another example, Defense indicated that standardization of hardware, software, and security architectures led to improved capability delivery and cyber security, and contributed to efficiency savings. Further, GSA reported that standardizing its enterprise document management solutions, simplifying its IT infrastructure, and improving information sharing to enable data-driven decision making had led to cost savings. In addition, the Departments of Veterans Affairs (VA) and Interior also reported successfully standardizing IT services to improve capability delivery and achieve cost savings.

The consolidation successes in achieving cost savings experienced by agencies indicate that they are making progress to realize the goals of

---

[40]See Pub. L. No. 112-81, § 2867, 125 Stat. 1298, 1704 (2011).

FDCCI. Further, many of these reported accomplishments directly relate to the four approaches to consolidating data centers—decommissioning, consolidation, cloud computing, and virtualization—discussed earlier in this report, thereby demonstrating that OMB's consolidation road map continues to provide a realistic means by which agencies can achieve cost savings.

Agencies Reported That Efforts to Achieve Consolidation Cost Savings Face Challenges Similar to Those Previously Reported

In 2011 and 2012, we reported[41] on the broad challenges that agencies were facing during data center consolidations. These included FDCCI-related, cultural, funding-related, operational, and technical challenges. In 2014, agencies reported that many of the same challenges still exist and impacted their ability to achieve cost savings through consolidation efforts. In addition, agencies identified many new challenges that were specific to achieving cost savings. As we found previously, some challenges are more common than others, with the most-reported challenge being faced by a total of eight agencies. One agency—HUD—did not report any challenges. Table 8 details the reported challenges and the numbers of agencies experiencing that challenge. The table is followed by a discussion of the most prevalent challenges.

---

[41]GAO-11-565 and GAO-12-742.

Table 8: Agency Consolidation Challenges in Achieving Cost Savings

Challenge type	Challenge	Number of agencies
Operational (31)	Gathering data from component agencies or organizations (e.g., data center inventories and cost savings)	6
	Determining costs and realizing savings when data centers are located in shared, multipurpose facilities	5
	Determining baseline costs of existing data center facilities from which to calculate savings	4
	Realizing significant cost savings from closure of smaller data centers (i.e., server rooms or closets)	2
	Using OMB's total cost of ownership model for planning consolidation savings	2
	Consolidation costs of upgrading services and infrastructure have exceeded savings	1
	Lack of suitable government-wide acquisition vehicles for cloud solutions	1
	Increasing vendor costs offset savings experienced through consolidation	1
	Contractual obligations, such as number of end-users supported, preclude the realization of savings through consolidation until those obligations end	1
	Coordinating internal and external entities involved in facilities, data center, and IT planning and related activities	1
	Making renovations required to repurpose office space delays savings	1
	Achieving savings from data center migration activities	1
	Relocating already consolidated hardware has not yielded cost savings	1
	Lack of finalized consolidation strategies and plans limited the agency to focusing on consolidating smaller facilities, thus preventing significant cost savings	1
	Consolidation activities will not be fully implemented until fiscal year 2016	1
	Consolidation efforts started prior to the Federal Data Center Consolidation Initiative make it difficult to identify and quantify savings	1
	Increasing demand for services offsets savings from consolidation	1
Technical (14)	Lack of electricity metering to determine power usage information	8
	Increased telecommunication costs after relocating small data centers or applications	2
	Relocating to enterprise data centers revealed system deficiencies that required additional costs to address (i.e., lack of disaster recovery)	1
	Need for significant systems engineering expertise and level of effort to take advantage of cost savings opportunities	1
	Physical hardware needs to be updated before savings from virtualizing legacy systems can be realized	1
	Readiness of systems, applications, and organizations to migrate to a shared infrastructure (i.e., enterprise data center)	1
Financial (14)	Obtaining the funding within their agency for consolidation efforts	8
	Structuring budget and accounting systems to account for individual data centers	6
Cultural (12)	Decentralized organizational structure was not geared toward consolidation	6
	Accepting cultural change that is part of consolidation	3
	Changing mission priorities	2
	Collaborating with other agencies to utilize excess capacity	1

Source: GAO analysis of agency data and interviews with agency officials. | GAO-14-713

Operational Challenges

Agencies reported that the most significant operational challenges included difficulty in obtaining information (such as data center inventory and cost savings data) from component organizations and determining costs and realizing savings when data centers were located in shared, multipurpose facilities. Specifically, 6 agencies reported that obtaining consolidation-related data from component organizations as a challenge to achieving cost savings which is similar to, but not as prevalent as, the 10 agencies we found having difficulty providing good quality asset inventories in 2012. For example, Defense's Data Center Consolidation Lead noted that getting component organizations to report all of their data centers remains a challenge in achieving cost savings, particularly in the case of smaller, single-server data centers (e.g., research stations or computers that are only used by a few individuals and are often not reported until replacement or enhancement is needed). Additionally, Agriculture's Associate CIO for Data Center Operations stated that it was often difficult to determine actual cost savings because the department's 32 component agencies did not track their total cost of IT, as portions are funded from many different sources versus being under the control of the component agency or office CIO (e.g., building rent and utilities, salaries, construction, etc.).

In addition, whereas we found in 2012 that one agency had difficulty with identifying and quantifying actual costs associated with data center facilities, we found that five agencies reported that it was difficult to determine costs and realized savings when data centers were located in shared, multipurpose facilities. For example, Energy reported that because several of its data centers were located in shared-use facilities, it was difficult for the department to determine the centers' total operating costs without an additional investment in advanced electricity metering. Energy also noted that it is difficult to determine the total cost savings and avoidances associated with the closure of these data centers until they are decommissioned and the vacated floor space is repurposed. EPA also reported that its data centers and server rooms were housed within mixed-use facilities, which generally cannot be discarded. Further, EPA expects that most former data center spaces will continue to provide local telecommunications and building access support services, which reduces potential substantive building operational cost reductions due to room decommissioning.

Technical Challenges

Agencies reported that the most significant technical challenges included a lack of electricity metering to determine power usage information and increased telecommunication costs after relocating small data centers or applications. The lack of electricity metering is similar to the difficulty we previously found for 15 agencies in 2012 with obtaining power usage information. Our current work found that 8 agencies reported that a lack of electricity metering to determine power usage was a challenge. For example, the Department of Labor (Labor) reported that a lack of electricity metering at many data centers prevented the department from accurately reporting energy savings attributed to the consolidation effort. Labor officials added that it was difficult to perform power usage efficiency calculations because the data to feed the calculations were not available.

As other examples, Transportation reported that its smaller data centers were operated in GSA-owned buildings which did not have electricity metering for the data center spaces. Transportation also noted that many of these spaces also contain telecommunications equipment which would remain after the data center equipment is relocated or decommissioned, which would mean the closures are not expected to produce significant savings. Further, NASA reported that it had encountered difficulties in metering its older, less-efficient facilities and that the modifications needed to make the facilities more efficient would require a significant amount of resources and yield a low return on investment. In addition, those modifications would adversely impact current operations due to the requisite power outages to install metering equipment. Commerce, Defense, Interior, NSF, and the Social Security Administration (SSA) also reported a lack of electricity metering as a challenge.

Regarding increased telecommunication costs, Interior and Transportation both reported this area as a challenge. Interior noted that the higher telecommunication premiums realized from its effort often offset the savings from consolidating a large number of small and closet-sized data centers. Transportation officials also stated that that the relocation of locally run applications to a consolidated data center may lead to increased telecommunications costs.

Financial Challenges

Agencies reported two financial challenges related to obtaining the funding required within their agency for consolidation efforts, as well as budget and accounting system issues that impacted their ability to achieve cost savings. In 2012, we found that nine agencies considered obtaining the funding required for consolidation and migration efforts to be a challenge. In 2014, eight agencies identified this challenge. For example, VA reported that the investment funding for all phases of its consolidation plan has not been available from the department as initially scheduled and, as a result has had to evolve its plan to address the risk of continued investment funding shortfalls so that it can continue to make progress towards its consolidation goals. In addition, SBA officials stated that a lack of funding allocated to implementing its data center consolidation strategy has been the primary challenge in achieving data center consolidation cost savings. Officials added that, in light of this challenge, the agency continues to examine federal cloud and GSA e-mail-as-a-service offerings, and initiated a request to the SBA investment governance process and a fiscal year 2015 request to pilot and migrate agency e-mail to a GSA vendor-managed cloud provider.

In addition, six agencies reported having budget and accounting systems that were not structured to account for individual data centers. For example, Energy officials stated that data centers have generally operated from separate facility and IT operations budgets and specific facility cost elements have not been tracked. In addition, officials added that different budgets are used to support different data centers, resulting in a lack of a consolidated budget for data centers, and has made documenting costs and related savings difficult. In addition, VA officials stated that IT costs often encompass multiple data centers and user facilities, making it challenging to parse the costs to the individual data centers and determine related savings.

Cultural Challenges

Agencies reported that the most significant cultural challenges included having a decentralized organizational structure that was not geared toward consolidation and accepting the cultural changes that were part of consolidation. In 2012, we found that two agencies encountered cultural challenges related to having a decentralized organization structure and five agencies had difficulty accepting cultural change as part of the consolidation effort. Our current work showed six agencies encountered cultural challenges related to having a decentralized organization structure. For example, GSA reported that its foremost challenge was that its data center costs and expenses were distributed across a federated organization. The agency indicated that the costs for rents; leases; personnel; and equipment repair, replacement, and service contracts were distributed across 11 regions, six components, and their subordinate organizations. Further, the Department of Justice (Justice) reported that its federated organizational structure had made it especially challenging to implement enterprise-wide initiatives such as data center consolidation. Officials noted that this was due, in part, to the need to build consensus for, plan, and then implement the consolidation changes, which does not happen quickly in a decentralized environment.

In addition, three agencies stated that accepting the cultural changes required to implement their consolidation efforts impacted their ability to achieve cost savings. For example, Justice also noted that its federated environment made it difficult for people to accept the cultural changes that are part of consolidation. Further, officials from Agriculture reported the challenge of accepting culture change as it encountered resistance to consolidation-related changes, including the use of cloud computing, from component agency personnel.

In any significant IT initiative, it is important that both successes and challenges be highlighted. In the case of FDCCI, a success highlights approaches and strategies that have helped agencies to achieve cost savings and fulfill the intent of the initiative. Conversely, a challenge identifies an area that was impacting an agency's ability to achieve cost savings and meet the intent of this government-wide effort. In light of how closely the successes and challenges reported by agencies relate to achieving cost savings—a key OMB goal for FDCCI—it will be important for OMB to continue to provide leadership and guidance to the initiative. This includes, as we have previously recommended, utilizing the Task Force—the primary organization responsible for supporting collaboration and knowledge transfer across the FDCCI agencies—to monitor and assist with agencies' consolidation efforts.[42]

---

[42]GAO-11-565.

Data Center Optimization Metrics and Related Targets Are Largely Established, but Key Area Not Addressed

Leading practices[43] have established the need for initiatives to develop performance measures to gauge progress. According to government and industry leading practices, performance measures should be measurable, outcome-oriented (i.e., identify targets for improving performance), and actively tracked and reported. In accordance with these principles, OMB's March 2013 memorandum[44] directed the Task Force to develop data center metrics for energy, facility, labor, storage, virtualization and cost per operating system to enable the measurement of the extent to which federal agency core data centers are optimized for total cost of ownership.

In May 2014, OMB released a set of 11 data center consolidation optimization metrics established by the Task Force.[45] These metrics address all of the categories defined in the March 2013 memorandum. In addition, related targets to be achieved by the end of fiscal year 2015 have been established for all the metrics except for the cost-per-operating-system metric, which provides for measuring progress on optimizing data center costs. According to a Task Force official, current data center inventory data (already required to be submitted by agencies on at least a yearly basis) will be used to calculate agencies' progress using the metrics and related targets. See table 9 for a list of the metrics, including the related category, a brief description, and the established target for each metric.

---

[43]GAO, *Aviation Weather: Agencies Need to Improve Performance Measurement and Fully Address Key Challenges*, GAO-10-843 (Washington, D.C.: Sept. 9, 2011); GAO, *NextGen Air Transportation System: FAA's Metrics Can Be Used to Report on Status of Individual Programs, but Not of Overall NextGen Implementation or Outcomes*, GAO-10-629 (Washington, D.C.: July 27, 2010); OMB, *Guide to the Program Assessment Rating Tool* (Washington, D.C.: January 2008); Department of the Navy, Office of the Chief Information Officer, *Guide for Developing and Using IT Performance Measurements* (Washington, D.C.: October 2001); and GSA, *Performance-Based Management: Eight Steps To Develop and Use Information Technology Performance Measures Effectively* (Washington, D.C.: 1996).

[44]OMB, Memorandum M-13-09.

[45]OMB, Memorandum M-14-08.

Table 9: Core Data Center Optimization Metrics and Targets

Metric	Metric category	Description	Target value (to be achieved by the end of FY 2015)
Power usage effectiveness	Energy	The amount of total power consumed at a facility divided by the total amount of IT power consumed.	1.5 or lower
Cost per operating system per hour	Cost per operating system	The total costs of a data center divided by the number of operating systems, figured for an hourly cost basis.	Not yet established[a]
Full-time equivalent ratio	Labor	The total number of servers divided by the total number of data center personnel (government and contract employees).	At least 25 servers per full-time equivalent
Facility utilization	Facility	The total number of server racks multiplied by 30 square feet and then divided by the total square feet reported in the data center.	At least 80 percent
Storage utilization	Storage	The total storage used divided by the total storage available.	75 percent for in-house storage utilization and/or 80 percent for cloud computing /outsourced facilities
Core to non-core physical server ratio	Facility	The number of physical servers in core data centers vs. the number of physical servers in non-core data centers.	At least 65 percent
Core to non-core operating system ratio	Virtualization	The number of operating systems in core data centers vs. the number of operating systems in non-core data centers.	At least 65 percent
Virtualized operating systems	Virtualization	The number of virtualized operating systems divided by the total number of operating systems.	75 percent of operating systems virtualized
Virtualization density	Virtualization	The number of virtual operating systems per virtual host.	10 operating systems per virtual host
Virtual hosts	Virtualization	The number of virtualized hosts divided by the total number of servers.	At least 20 percent
Virtualization optimization percent	Virtualization	Average of the preceding three metrics: virtualized operating systems, virtualization density, and virtual hosts.	Not applicable—average of the three metrics above

Source: GAO analysis of OMB and Task Force data. | GAO-14-713

[a]According to OMB staff, this target is expected to be finalized in the fall of 2014.

According to OMB staff from the Office of E-Government and Information Technology, there have been challenges in reaching consensus on the cost-per-operating-system target. Specifically, the staff stated that the Task Force has had difficulty with developing a baseline for cloud computing costs that could be used to establish an appropriate target because private sector cloud providers are continually cutting the prices for their services. Development of the cost-per-operating-system target is expected to continue and OMB staff stated that the Task Force expects to finalize the target in the fall of 2014.

In addition, although low server utilization rates were a driving force cited by OMB in launching FDCCI, the new data center optimization metrics do not address this key issue. As previously mentioned, in 2009, OMB reported[46] that server utilization rates were as low as 5 percent across the federal government's servers. OMB subsequently required agencies to report on server utilization percentage as part of their 2011 and 2012 consolidation plans and included a suggested target of 60 to 70 percent server utilization in its 2011 and 2012 FDCCI consolidation plan guidance. OMB later eliminated the requirement for agencies to continue to update their consolidation plans, but indicated in its March 2013 memorandum[47] that it would continue tracking agencies' progress through other means, including the data center optimization metrics.

However, a metric for server utilization was not included in the final metrics established by the Task Force. According to an official from the GSA FDCCI Program Management Office that led initial efforts to establish the metrics, server utilization was not included as a metric for a variety of reasons, including that agencies have not traditionally collected the necessary data to be able to calculate server utilization, agencies do not have the server monitoring capabilities required to collect such data, and improvements in other areas of the metrics (such as virtualization) would likely result in higher server utilization. However, as previously mentioned, with server utilization a driving factor for FDCCI and measuring as low as 5 percent as recently as 2009, determining progress against this metric is critical to improving the efficiency, performance, and environmental footprint of federal data center activities.

Without an established target for one of its key cost metrics, the cost per operating system, OMB may not be getting complete information about agencies' progress in their data center optimization efforts and, therefore, may be lacking important insight that limits its ability to take corrective actions as needed. In addition, without a specific metric for server

---

[46]OMB, *Inventory of Federal Data Center Activity*, Budget Data Request No. 09-41 (Washington, D.C.: Aug. 10, 2009).

[47]OMB, Memorandum M-13-09.

utilization, OMB may not be fully aware of agencies' progress on a key metric that was a driving force in launching FDCCI.

Conclusions

After slightly more than 4 years into FDCCI, agencies have begun to report significant savings from their consolidation efforts—most notably, Defense, DHS, and Treasury, which account for 74 percent of the reported savings to date. Furthermore, with approximately $3.3 billion in total planned savings being reported by agencies through fiscal year 2015, meeting OMB's savings goal is increasingly more likely and, if executed as planned, would represent a significant accomplishment for OMB and the FDCCI agencies. However, limited or no savings achieved at agencies with major consolidation efforts underway suggests that additional actions are necessary. OMB's and these agencies' continued efforts to address challenges and identify cost savings opportunities, through the use of such existing mechanisms as PortfolioStat sessions, will result in even more savings. Additionally, agencies' continued underreporting of consolidation savings will limit OMB's ability to accurately track agencies' progress and report to Congress, a point highlighted by the significant understatement of agency-reported savings—by approximately $622 million through fiscal year 2013—in OMB's recent congressional submission, and—by over $2.2 billion through fiscal year 2015—in agency data submissions to OMB.

As the federal consolidation effort has matured over the past few years, agencies have reported noteworthy successes in achieving cost savings—particularly in leveraging virtualization and cloud computing as a means to achieve such savings. These constructive experiences, which stem from OMB's recommended consolidation strategies, indicate that FDCCI is moving in the right direction. However, as agencies work toward achieving their cost savings goals, many continue to report challenges related to gathering the necessary technical information from which to calculate savings and funding the consolidation itself. While these challenges are consistent with those reported in the past, others, such as determining savings when data centers are located in multipurpose facilities, have become more prominent. Such a dynamic environment reinforces the need for agencies to remain in communication with OMB in order to facilitate knowledge sharing and transfer and for OMB to continue to provide leadership and guidance, as we have previously recommended.

OMB's May 2014 publication of the data center optimization metrics is a considerable step forward in helping OMB provide better oversight of agencies' efforts to optimize their core data centers. Furthermore, targets established for nearly all the metrics will provide agencies with clear and transparent goals to guide their data center optimization efforts. However, the continued absence of a metric for server utilization, despite OMB's previously-reported concerns about low average utilization rates, represents a missed opportunity to track agencies' progress on this metric. In the absence of such a metric, OMB will be challenged in demonstrating agencies' improvement in an area that was a driving force in starting FDCCI and which is critical to improving the efficiency, performance, and environmental footprint of federal data center activities.

Recommendations for Executive Action

To better ensure that FDCCI improves governmental efficiency and achieves cost savings, we are making two recommendations to OMB. We recommend that the Director of OMB direct the Federal CIO to:

- utilize the existing PortfolioStat review sessions to assist HHS, Interior, Justice, Labor, GSA, and NASA in identifying data center consolidation cost savings opportunities; and

- as part of any future evaluation of the data center optimization metrics, develop and implement a metric for server utilization.

We also recommend that the Secretaries of HHS, the Interior, Justice, and Labor, and the Administrators of GSA and NASA complete action plans for addressing their challenges in reporting cost savings, as discussed in this report.

Finally, we recommend that the Secretaries of Agriculture, Commerce, Defense, Energy, the Interior, Transportation, the Treasury, and VA; the Administrators of EPA and NASA; and the Director of the Office of Personnel Management direct responsible officials to report all data center consolidation cost savings and avoidances to OMB in accordance with established guidance.

Agency Comments and Our Evaluation

We received comments on a draft of our report from OMB, the 15 agencies to which we made recommendations, and the other 9 agencies mentioned in the report. Specifically, OMB and 12 agencies agreed with our recommendations, 1 agency did not state whether it agreed or disagreed, 1 agency had no comments, and 1 agency—NASA—agreed with one of our recommendations but partially agreed with the other. The other 9 agencies had no specific comments on our recommendations.

Multiple agencies also provided technical comments, which we incorporated as appropriate. Each of the agency's comments are discussed in more detail below.

- In comments provided by e-mail on July 30, 2014, a policy analyst from OMB's Office of E-Government and Information Technology stated that OMB agreed with the findings and recommendations of the report. OMB also provided technical comments, which we have incorporated as appropriate.

- In comments provided by e-mail, a liaison officer from Agriculture's Office of the CIO stated that the department agreed with the report's recommendation and noted steps planned to address the recommendation, including engaging with Agriculture agencies to collect actual cost savings and avoidance information realized through their internal consolidation efforts. In addition, the department noted that the Office of the CIO is drafting a Cloud Computing Departmental Directive that, in addition to other requirements, is expected to standardize the process by which IT investments are evaluated for cloud services, including projected and actual cost savings and avoidances.

- In written comments, Commerce's Deputy Secretary stated that the department concurred with the general findings of the report as they applied to Commerce. The department did not state whether it agreed or disagreed with our recommendation, but noted that department would ensure that all savings and avoidances identified by its component bureaus are reported through OMB's integrated data collection. Commerce's written comments are provided in appendix II.

- Our draft report provided to Defense for comment included a recommendation that the department complete an action plan for addressing their challenges in reporting cost savings. This was based on the department withdrawing its original savings figures—totaling approximately $4.7 billion between fiscal years 2011 through 2017—reported earlier in our review, and submitting revised figures using a new methodology that did not result in planned cost savings estimates beyond fiscal year 2014. Subsequently, Defense provided additional documentation of its planned savings between fiscal years 2015 and 2017, which resulted in an updated total planned cost savings figure of approximately $2.6 billion between fiscal years 2011 and 2017. As a result of Defense's action, we have removed this recommendation from our report. We have also made changes to the report to reflect these newly-reported numbers. However, in reviewing the additional cost savings information provided by the department, we found that Defense had not fully reported its fiscal years 2012 through 2015 cost savings to OMB, consistent with OMB guidance. As a result, we have added a recommendation for Defense to report all data center consolidation cost savings and avoidances to OMB in accordance with established guidance.

In written comments, Defense's Acting Principal Deputy CIO stated that the department agreed with the amended report and recommendation. Defense's written comments are provided in appendix III.

- In written comments, Energy's CIO stated that the department concurred with the report's recommendation and noted steps being taken by the department to address the discrepancies in its reporting of estimated cost savings and avoidances. For example, the CIO stated that, in order to improve the accuracy and completeness of the data center cost savings and avoidance data, the Energy will clarify its guidance for the integrated data collection data call to better ensure that the department's organizations report on all data center optimization and consolidation activities. Energy's written comments are provided in appendix IV.

- In comments provided by e-mail on August 25, 2014, an official from HHS's Division for Oversight and Investigations, Assistant Secretary for Legislation, stated that the department concurred with the report's recommendation.

- In comments provided by e-mail on August 11, 2014, an Interior OIG/GAO Audit Liaison stated that the department concurred with the report's findings and recommendations.

- In comments provided by e-mail on August 20, 2014, a Justice audit liaison stated that the department concurred with the report's recommendation.

- In written comments, Labor's Assistant Secretary for Administration and Management and CIO stated that the department concurred with the report's recommendations. The department also provided technical comments, including stating that Labor's data center inventory figures in our draft report were incorrect. Specifically, the department asserted that its total number of data centers was lower than the number cited in our report and that its number of closed data centers was higher. However, the department did not provide supporting documentation for these changes. We have incorporated Labor's other technical comment related to its challenges in achieving cost reductions. Labor's written comments are provided in appendix V.

- In written comments, Transportation's Assistant Secretary for Administration stated that the department agreed with the recommendation related to reporting all of its data center consolidation cost savings and avoidances to OMB, but asserted that the department's current reporting of this information satisfied our recommendation. While we acknowledge in our report that Transportation has reported a portion of its cost savings and avoidances to OMB, we identified discrepancies between that information and the cost savings and avoidance information that the department reported to us. As a result, we determined that Transportation's savings and avoidances were not being fully reported to OMB. Therefore, we continue to believe that our recommendation remains valid. Transportation's written comments are provided in appendix VI.

- In written comments, Treasury's Acting Deputy Assistant Secretary for Information Systems and CIO stated that Treasury had no comments on the report. Treasury's written comments are provided in appendix VII.

- In written comments, VA's Chief of Staff stated that the department concurred with our recommendation to report all data center consolidation cost savings and avoidances to OMB, stating that it plans to begin reporting this information by the end of 2014, but strongly disagreed with our recommendation that OMB include server utilization in the FDCCI metrics. In our report, we acknowledge the reasons that the server utilization metric was not included when OMB issued the data center optimization metrics in May 2014, such as lack of agency data to calculate utilization and lack of utilization monitoring capabilities. However, because low server utilization rates were a driving force in launching FDCCI, we believe that tracking this metric can provide useful information in assessing agencies' progress in optimizing their data centers. As previously mentioned, OMB agreed with our findings and recommendations related to this area. Accordingly, we continue to believe our recommendation remains valid. VA's written comments are provided in appendix VIII.

- In written comments, EPA's Acting Assistant Administrator and CIO stated that the agency agreed with our findings, conclusions, and recommendation, and noted processes in place to address the recommendation. EPA's written comments are provided in appendix IX.

- In written comments, GSA's Administrator stated that the agency agreed with the report's findings and recommendation and would take appropriate actions to address the recommendation. GSA's written comments are provided in appendix X.

- In written comments, NASA's CIO stated that the agency concurred with one of two of our recommendations and partially concurred with the other. Specifically, NASA agreed with our recommendation related to reporting all of its data center consolidation cost savings and avoidances to OMB, stating that it would issue a directive by October 2014. The agency partially concurred with our recommendation to complete an action plan for addressing challenges in reporting cost savings. Specifically, NASA stated that, while it plans to develop and finalize revisions of existing action plans by December 2014, execution of those plans remains a challenge due to difficulties in power metering, particularly in older multipurpose buildings, and measuring facility savings. While we acknowledge the challenges described by NASA in our report, we believe that completing an action plan to address these challenges, as we recommended, could serve as a valuable tool in defining a road map toward overcoming these issues. We therefore continue to believe our recommendation remains valid. NASA's written comments are provided in appendix XI.

- In written comments, OPM's CIO stated that the agency concurred with our recommendation and described planned actions to address our recommendation. For example, the CIO stated that OPM is preparing its data center consolidation plan to include consideration for shared services and cloud technologies and that any related cost savings will be reported once the consolidation plan is implemented. OPM's written comments are provided in appendix XII.

- In comments provided via e-mail on August 5, 2014, a policy analyst from Education's Office of the Secretary/Executive Secretariat stated that the department had no comments on the report.

- In comments provided via e-mail on August 18, 2014, a program analyst from DHS's Departmental GAO-OIG Liaison Office stated that the department had no technical comments on the report.

- In written comments, HUD's CIO stated that the agency had no comments on the report. HUD's written comments are provided in appendix XIII.

- In comments provided by e-mail on August 8, 2014, a senior management analyst from State's Bureau of the Comptroller and Global Financial Services stated that the agency had no comments on the report.

- In written comments, NSF's CIO stated that the agency had no comments on the report. NSF's written comments are provided in appendix XIV.

- In comments provided via e-mail on August 19, 2014, an executive technical assistant from NRC's Office of the Executive Director for Operations stated that the agency had no comments on the report.

- In comments provided via e-mail on August 12, 2014, the program manager for SBA's Office of Congressional and Legislative Affairs stated that the agency had no comments on the report.

- In written comments, the Deputy Chief of Staff from SSA's Office of the Commissioner stated that the agency had no comments on the report. SSA's written comments are provided in appendix XV.

- In comments provided via e-mail on August 11, 2014, a systems accountant from USAID's Office of the Chief Financial Officer, Audit, Performance and Compliance Division, stated that the agency had no comments on the report.

We are sending copies of this report to interested congressional committees, the Director of OMB, the secretaries and agency heads of the departments and agencies addressed in this report, and other interested parties. In addition, the report will be available at no charge on GAO's website at http://www.gao.gov.

If you or your staffs have any questions on the matters discussed in this report, please contact me at (202) 512-9286 or pownerd@gao.gov.

Contact points for our Offices of Congressional Relations and Public Affairs may be found on the last page of this report. GAO staff who made major contributions to this report are listed in appendix XVI.

David A. Powner
Director, Information Technology
Management Issues

List of requesters

The Honorable Thomas R. Carper
Chairman
The Honorable Tom A. Coburn, M.D.
Ranking Member
Committee on Homeland Security and Governmental Affairs
United States Senate

The Honorable Darrell Issa
Chairman
The Honorable Elijah E. Cummings
Ranking Member
Committee on Oversight and Government Reform
House of Representatives

The Honorable John L. Mica
Chairman
The Honorable Gerald E. Connolly
Ranking Member
Subcommittee on Government Operations
Committee on Oversight and Government Reform
House of Representatives

Appendix I: Objectives, Scope, and Methodology

Our objectives were to (1) evaluate the extent to which agencies have achieved cost savings to date and identified future savings through their consolidation efforts, (2) identify agencies' notable consolidation successes and challenges in achieving cost savings, and (3) evaluate the extent to which data center optimization metrics have been established.

To evaluate the extent to which agencies have achieved cost savings to date and identified future savings through their consolidation efforts, we obtained and analyzed cost savings and avoidance documentation, relative to requirements of the Office of Management and Budget's (OMB) March 2013 memorandum,[1] from the 24 departments and agencies (agencies) in our review.[2] This documentation included, but was not limited to, agencies' quarterly reports of cost savings and avoidances submitted to OMB, total cost of ownership[3] models, contract and budget documentation, and internal agency status reports. To determine cost savings achieved to date, we totaled agency reported savings and avoidances from fiscal years 2011 through 2013, and to identify future planned savings we totaled agency projected savings and avoidances from fiscal years 2014 through 2017.[4] We also compared agencies' cost savings and avoidance information to key requirements for identifying and reporting data center consolidation cost savings and avoidances, as outlined in OMB's March 2013 memorandum.

To assess the reliability of agencies' cost savings and avoidance data, we reviewed related documentation provided by agency data center program

---

[1] OMB, *Fiscal Year 2013 PortfolioStat Guidance: Strengthening Federal IT Portfolio Management*, Memorandum M-13-09 (Washington, D.C.: Mar. 27, 2013).

[2] The 24 major departments and agencies that participate in the Federal Data Center Consolidation Initiative are the Departments of Agriculture, Commerce, Defense, Education, Energy, Health and Human Services, Homeland Security, Housing and Urban Development, the Interior, Justice, Labor, State, Transportation, the Treasury, and Veterans Affairs; the Environmental Protection Agency, General Services Administration, National Aeronautics and Space Administration, National Science Foundation, Nuclear Regulatory Commission, Office of Personnel Management, Small Business Administration, Social Security Administration, and U.S. Agency for International Development.

[3] OMB refers to total cost of ownership as all associated data center-related activities and costs without regard to ownership, project association, or funding line.

[4] Three agencies—the Department of Housing and Urban Development, the Small Business Administration, and the U.S. Agency for International Development—reported no cost savings to date or planned future savings.

managers and other cognizant officials, such as agency total cost of ownership models, agency-developed spreadsheets, agencies' quarterly data submissions to OMB, among other sources. We also compared the cost savings and avoidances reported to us by agencies with cost savings identified in OMB's quarterly reports to Congress on the status of information technology reform efforts.[5] In addition, we reviewed agency documentation for missing data or other errors (e.g., incorrect calculations). Finally, we interviewed agency officials to obtain additional supporting information regarding how their cost savings and avoidance figures were determined, the processes and methods to recalculate the figures, and the steps that the agency took to ensure the reliability of their figures and validate their figures. We also discussed with agency officials any discrepancies or potential errors identified during our review of their supporting documentation to determine the cause or request additional information. We determined that the data were sufficiently reliable to report on agencies' cost savings achieved to date and identified future savings. However, as part of our reliability assessment, we identified issues with the reliability of OMB's quarterly reports to Congress, including that agencies' data center consolidation cost savings were not being fully reflected in OMB's report. We have highlighted this issue in our report.

Lastly, we reviewed agencies' data center facility reductions as reported on http://data.gov and compared the information to agencies' cost savings and avoidances achieved to date, taking into consideration the challenges in achieving savings identified by agencies. To assess the reliability of agencies' data center reductions, we reviewed prior reporting of data center closures to check for anomalies in the data, such as fewer closures for agencies in more recent data sets than previously reported. We also checked for missing data, outliers, and other obvious errors, such as missing closure status information. Finally, we interviewed OMB staff from the Office of E-Government and Information Technology regarding actions taken to verify the data. We determined that the data were sufficiently reliable to report on agencies' consolidation progress.

To identify notable consolidation successes and challenges in achieving cost savings, we reviewed agencies' cost savings documentation,

---

[5]OMB, *Quarterly Report to Congress: Information Technology Oversight and Reform* (Washington, D.C.: May 6, 2014) and *Quarterly Report to Congress: Integrated, Efficient, and Effective Uses of Information Technology* (Washington, D.C.: Feb. 18, 2014).

including quarterly reports on cost savings and avoidances submitted to OMB, total cost of ownership models, contract and budget documentation, internal agency status reports, and other documentation, and interviewed agency officials. To determine the types of successes experienced, we identified areas reported in agencies' documentation with directly attributable cost savings or avoidances. We also interviewed agency officials to identify additional successes in achieving cost savings, including areas where the agency may not have been able to quantify the savings. To determine challenges in achieving cost savings, we interviewed agency officials to obtain information regarding challenges faced, as well as to discuss any steps taken, or planned, to address the challenges identified. We then determined which successes and challenges were encountered most often. In some cases, agencies' cost savings and avoidance data were used to highlight the impact of a particular success. As a result of the reliability assessment performed for our first objective, we determined these data to be sufficiently reliable for reporting on agencies' cost savings and avoidances achieved to date and planned.

To evaluate the extent to which data center optimization metrics have been established, we analyzed OMB's March 2013 memorandum[6] to determine OMB's requirements for such metrics, including the responsibilities for completing the metrics and the key areas or categories that were to be addressed by the metrics. We then compared OMB's requirements for the metrics to the final metrics, as documented in a May 2014 OMB memorandum.[7] We also reviewed previous data center consolidation-related OMB memorandums[8] and consolidation plan guidance to identify metrics that had previously been identified by OMB as indicators of data center optimization success and determined the extent to which the metrics addressed these areas. Finally, we interviewed relevant OMB, General Services Administration, and Data Center Consolidation Task Force officials to discuss the process by which

---

[6]OMB, Memorandum M-13-09.

[7]OMB, *Fiscal Year 2014 PortfolioStat*, Memorandum M-14-08 (Washington, D.C.: May 7, 2014).

[8]See, for example, OMB, *Update on the Federal Data Center Consolidation Initiative* (Washington, D.C.: Oct. 1, 2010); *Federal Data Center Consolidation Initiative* (Washington, D.C.: Feb. 26, 2010); and *Inventory of Federal Data Center Activity*, Budget Data Request No. 09-41 (Washington, D.C.: Aug. 10, 2009).

the metrics were established and to determine the extent that related
targets, or goals, for the metrics had been established.

We conducted this performance audit from October 2013 to September
2014 in accordance with generally accepted government auditing
standards. Those standards require that we plan and perform the audit to
obtain sufficient, appropriate evidence to provide a reasonable basis for
our findings and conclusions based on our audit objectives. We believe
that the evidence obtained provides a reasonable basis for our findings
and conclusions based on our audit objectives.

Appendix II: Comments from the Department of Commerce

THE DEPUTY SECRETARY OF COMMERCE
Washington, D.C. 20230

August 19, 2014

Mr. David A. Powner
Director, Information Technology Management Issues
U.S. Government Accountability Office
441 G Street NW
Washington, DC 20548

Dear Mr. Powner:

Thank you for the opportunity to review and comment on the Government Accountability Office draft report entitled *Reporting Can Be Improved to Reflect Substantial Planned Savings* (GAO-14-713).

We concur with the general findings as they apply to the Department of Commerce. Regarding the specific recommendation relating to the Department's reporting all cost savings and avoidances resulting from data center consolidation, we will ensure that all cost savings and cost avoidances identified by our component bureaus are reported through the Office of Management and Budget's integrated data collection.

If you have any questions, please contact Jerry Harper, Director, Office of IT Policy and Planning, at 202-482-0222.

Sincerely,

Bruce H. Andrews

Appendix III: Comments from the Department of Defense

DEPARTMENT OF DEFENSE
6000 DEFENSE PENTAGON
WASHINGTON, D.C. 20301-6000

CHIEF INFORMATION OFFICER

SEP 0 8 2014

Mr. David A. Powner
Director, Information Technology Management Issues
U.S. Government Accountability Office
441 G Street, NW
Washington DC 20548

Dear Mr. Powner:

This is the Department of Defense (DoD) response to the GAO Draft Report GAO-14-713, "DATA CENTER CONSOLIDATION: Reporting Can Be Improved to Reflect Substantial Planned Savings," dated July 18, 2014 (GAO Code 311294).

The Department concurs with the report as amended and with the recommendation provided to the Secretary of Defense.

The point of contact for this matter is Bob Brown at email: james.r.brown632.civ@mail.mil, 571-372-4445.

Sincerely,

David L. Devries
Principal Deputy
Acting

Appendix IV: Comments from the Department of Energy

Department of Energy
Washington, DC 20585

August 14, 2014

Mr. David A. Powner
Director, Information Technology Management Issues
U.S. Government Accountability Office
441 G Street, NW
Washington, DC 20548

Dear Mr. Powner:

The Department of Energy's (DOE or "Energy") Office of the Chief Information Officer (OCIO) appreciates the opportunity to provide comments to the Government Accountability Office's (GAO) Draft Report, *Data Center Consolidation: Reporting Can Be Improved to Reflect Substantial Planned Savings* (GAO-14-713).

Management Response to Audit Findings/Comments

The "Recommendations for Executive Action" of the report state the DOE should *"report all data center consolidation cost savings and avoidance to OMB in accordance with established guidance."* Consistent with OMB guidance, memorandum M-14-08, May 2014, the DOE PortfolioStat Integrated Data Collection (IDC) process is now the official method for reporting data center cost savings / avoidance data.

The report documents in Table 6, that DOE is only "Partially" reporting savings and avoidance dollars per the discrepancy between the numbers "Reported to GAO" and the "Integrated Data Collection Process." The estimated savings and cost avoidance data provided to GAO in April 2014 were collected from an ad-hoc Federal Data Center Consolidation Initiative (FDCCI) data call in April 2014, prior to the PortfolioStat IDC data call conducted in May 2014. Reconciliation of the two data calls was not sufficiently conducted, resulting in the identified discrepancies between the two reports.

Management Response to Recommendation

Recommendation to the Secretary of Energy: Report all data center consolidation cost savings and avoidance to OMB in accordance with established guidance.

DOE concurs with the recommendation.

1) Consistent with OMB guidance, memorandum M-14-08, May 2014, the PortfolioStat IDC Consolidated Cost Savings and Avoidance report is now considered the official and only method for reporting savings and cost avoidance from data center consolidation and optimization efforts. While the FDCCI inventory and data center closing status updates have been integrated with the

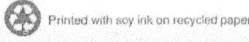
Printed with soy ink on recycled paper

2

PortfolioStat IDC data call process, that data will be reported to OMB via the FDCCI Customer Portal.

2) To improve the accuracy and completeness of the data center savings and cost avoidance data, DOE will clarify the guidance issued for the PortfolioStat IDC data call, ensuring DOE organizations report on all data center optimization and consolidation activities.

Thank you for the opportunity to review this report. If you have any questions related to this letter, please feel free to contact me at (202) 586-0166.

Sincerely,

Robert F. Brese
Chief Information Officer

Appendix V: Comments from the Department of Labor

U.S. Department of Labor　　Office of the Assistant Secretary
for Administration and Management
Washington, D.C. 20210

AUG 1 4 2014

Mr. David A. Powner
Director
Information Technology Management Issues
Government Accountability Office
441 G Street, NW
Washington, D.C. 20548

Dear Mr. Powner:

Thank you for the opportunity to review draft GAO Report (GAO-14-713): *Data Center Consolidation – Reporting Can Be Improved to Reflect Substantial Planned Savings.* The Department of Labor concurs with GAO's recommendations. The following are technical comments:

- Page 11 – The metrics (as of May 2014) are incorrect.
  - The Department has 8 core data centers, not 9.
  - DOL has 71 non-core data centers, not 84.
  - DOL has 79 data centers, not 93.
  - DOL has closed 18 data centers (11%).
- Page 25 – additional comment
  - We would like to add to our statement that there is a facilities and procurement driven lag between the time the data center is closed and cost reductions can be realized.

Should you have any questions regarding the Department's response, please contact Dawn Leaf, Deputy Chief Information Officer, at (202) 693-4200 or leaf.dawn.m@dol.gov.

Sincerely,

T. Michael Kerr
Assistant Secretary for Administration and Management,
Chief Information Officer

Appendix VI: Comments from the Department of Transportation

U.S. Department
of Transportation

Office of the Secretary
of Transportation

Assistant Secretary
for Administration

1200 New Jersey Avenue, SE
Washington, DC 20590

AUG 1 3 2014

David A. Powner
Director of Information Management
 and Technology Resources
U.S. Government Accountability Office
441 G Street NW
Washington, DC 20548

Re: DOT Comments on GAO draft report - Data Center Consolidation (GAO-14-713)

The Department of Transportation (DOT) continues to make great strides in reducing its data center footprint. Our data center consolidation goal is to make additional improvements to our IT asset utilization, achieve cost savings, reduce our energy consumption, and optimize space utilization. Additionally, the Department benefits from specific programmatic metrics to drive achievement in Power Utilization, Cost/OS/hr, Virtualization, FTE Ratio, Facility Utilization, Storage Utilization, Clould Utilization and Core to Non-Core server and OS rations. These efforts, in collaboration with our Operating Administrations (OAs), enable the Department to achieve further savings and efficiencies.

- As required, DOT Chief Information Officer (CIO) reports the data center consolidation cost savings and avoidance information on a quarterly basis to the Office of Management and Budget (OMB) through their Intergrated Data Collection (IDC) website. This current practice satisfies the recommendation made to the Department and should be considered closed upon issuance of the GAO report.
- Internally, DOT continues efforts to further consolidate and find cost savings or avoid costs all together.

Upon preliminary review of the recommendation, DOT agrees with the recommendation provided in the report. The Department will provide a detailed response to the recommendation within 60 days of the GAO report issuance.

We appreciate this opportunity to offer additional perspective on the GAO report. Please contact Martin Gertel, Director of Audit Relations, at (202) 366-4986 with any questions or for additional details about these comments.

Sincerely,

Brodi Fontenot
Assistant Secretary for Administration

Appendix VII: Comments from the Department of the Treasury

DEPARTMENT OF THE TREASURY
WASHINGTON, D.C.

AUG 1 8 2014

Mr. David A. Powner
Director
Information Technology Management Issues
U.S. Government Accountability Office
441 G Street, NW
Washington, DC 20548

Dear Mr. Powner,

Thank you for the opportunity to provide comments on GAO's Draft Report, *"Data Center Consolidation: Reporting Can Be Improved to Reflect Substantial Planned Savings (GAO-14-713)."* The Department of the Treasury has no comments on the Report and appreciates GAO's efforts in its development.

Please contact me at 202-622-1200 if you need anything further.

Sincerely,

For Mike Parker
Acting Deputy Assistant Secretary for Information
Systems and Chief Information Officer

Appendix VIII: Comments from the Department of Veterans Affairs

DEPARTMENT OF VETERANS AFFAIRS
WASHINGTON DC 20420

August 18, 2014

Mr. David A. Powner
Director, Information Technology
  Management Issues
U.S. Government Accountability Office
441 G Street, NW
Washington, DC 20548

Dear Mr. Powner:

The Department of Veterans Affairs (VA) has reviewed the Government Accountability Office's (GAO) draft report, *"DATA CENTER CONSOLIDATION: Reporting Can Be Improved to Reflect Substantial Planned Savings"* (GAO-14-713). VA generally agrees with GAO's conclusions; however, we strongly disagree with GAO's recommendation that the Office of Management and Budget include server utilization in the Federal Data Center Consolidation Initiative metrics. VA concurs with GAO's recommendation to the Department.

The enclosure specifically addresses GAO's recommendation to VA in the draft report and provides general comments to the draft report. VA appreciates the opportunity to comment on your draft report.

Sincerely,

Jose D. Riojas
Chief of Staff

Enclosure

Department of Veterans Affairs (VA) Response to
Government Accountability Office (GAO) Draft Report
*"DATA CENTER CONSOLIDATION: Reporting Can Be Improved to Reflect
Substantial Planned Savings"*
(GAO-14-713)

GAO Recommendation: The Secretary of Veterans Affairs direct responsible
officials to report all data center consolidation cost savings and avoidances to
OMB in accordance with established guidance.

VA Comment: Concur. The Department of Veterans Affairs plans to begin reporting
data center consolidation cost savings and avoidances to the Office of Management
and Budget via PortfolioStat by the end of 2014.

1

Appendix IX: Comments from the Environmental Protection Agency

UNITED STATES ENVIRONMENTAL PROTECTION AGENCY
WASHINGTON, D.C. 20460

AUG 1 4 2014

David A. Powner
Director, Information Technology Management Issues
U.S. Government Accountability Office
441 G Street, NW
Washington, DC 20548

OFFICE OF
ENVIRONMENTAL INFORMATION

Dear Mr. Powner:

Thank you for the opportunity to review and comment on GAO's draft report, "Data Center Consolidation – Reporting Can Be Improved to Reflect Substantial Planned Savings," GAO-14-713. The purpose of this letter is to provide the Environmental Protection Agency's (EPA) response to your recommendation. The EPA agrees with the GAO's findings, conclusions, and recommendation.

The GAO draft report reviews federal agencies continuing efforts to consolidate their data centers and achieve cost savings. EPA generally agrees with the GAO recommendations as outlined below.

GAO Recommendation

We recommend that ... the Administrator of EPA ... direct responsible officials to report all data center consolidation cost savings and avoidances to OMB in accordance with established guidance.

EPA Response:

EPA generally agrees with the recommendation as follows:
- EPA has been reporting data center consolidation cost savings as part of the quarterly OMB PortfolioStat Integrated Data Call (IDC) submission.
- In the process of preparing the quarterly IDC submissions, a data call is issued to the officials at EPA's National Computing Center who are responsible for the data center consolidation. They provide the cost saving data. This process will continue for future iterations of the data call.

Thank you for the opportunity to review and comment on GAO's draft report. If you have questions, please contact Fawn Freeman at 202-564-2762.

Sincerely,

Renee P. Wynn
Acting Assistant Administrator and Chief Information Officer

cc: Harrell Watkins, Acting Director, OTOP
     Bob Trent, EPA Liaison Team Lead
     Mark Howard, EPA Liaison Team
     Pat Williams, OEI
     Anne Mangiafico, OTOP

cc: Harrell Watkins, Acting Director, OTOP
       Bob Trent, EPA Liaison Team Lead
       Mark Howard, EPA Liaison Team
       Pat Williams, OEI
       Anne Mangiafico, OTOP
       Fawn Freeman, OTOP

2

Appendix X: Comments from the General Services Administration

GSA Administrator

August 20, 2014

The Honorable Gene L. Dodaro
Comptroller General of the United States
U.S. Government Accountability Office
Washington, DC 20548

Dear Mr. Dodaro:

The U.S. General Services Administration (GSA) appreciates the opportunity to review and comment on the draft report, *Data Center Consolidation: Reporting Can Be Improved to Reflect Substantial Planned Savings*, (GAO-14-713). The U.S. Government Accountability Office (GAO) recommends that the GSA Administrator:

- Complete action plans for addressing their challenges in reporting cost savings as discussed in the report.

We agree with the findings and recommendation and will take appropriate action. If you have any questions or concerns, please do not hesitate to contact me at (202) 501-0800, or Ms. Lisa Austin, Associate Administrator, Office of Congressional and Intergovernmental Affairs, at (202) 501-0563.

Sincerely,

Dan Tangherlini
Administrator

cc: David A. Powner, Director, Information Technology Management Issues, GAO

U.S. General Services Administration
1800 F Street, NW
Washington, DC 20405-0002
www.gsa.gov

Appendix XI: Comments from the National Aeronautics and Space Administration

National Aeronautics and Space Administration

Headquarters
Washington, DC 20546-0001

AUG 1 8 2014

Reply to Attn of: Office of the Chief Information Officer

Mr. David Powner
Director
Information Technology Management Issues
United States Government Accountability Office
Washington, DC 20548

Dear Mr. Powner:

The National Aeronautics and Space Administration (NASA) appreciates the opportunity to review and comment on the Government Accountability Office (GAO) draft report entitled, "DATA CENTER CONSOLIDATION Reporting Can Be Improved to Reflect Substantial Planned Savings" (GAO-14-713).

In the draft report, GAO addresses two recommendations to the NASA Administrator. To ensure the Agency fully reports its consolidation cost savings, GAO recommends the following actions:

Recommendation 1: Complete action plans for addressing challenges in reporting cost savings, as discussed in the report.

Management's Response: NASA partially concurs. While the final development and revision of existing action plans can be completed by December 31, 2014, execution of these plans remains a challenge, based on limited availability of funds for both data center consolidation and power monitoring. NASA continues to spend resources to find cost effective ways to meter the data centers better, while recognizing the investment cost of metering erodes the savings. To meet this recommendation, in addition to funding limitations, as described to GAO and written in the report, there are challenges in obtaining actuals for many reporting elements. NASA's data centers are rooms in older multi-purpose buildings. The buildings are not metered at the room level and the aging electrical and mechanical infrastructure is not designed to have meters inserted. Regarding facilities savings, the facility maintenance cost is not measured by data center. When a data center is closed or footprint reduced, the space does not go away; rather it remains on the Agency's inventory and is repurposed. The best reporting that can be obtained from most of these facilities is estimates. The best estimating tool available was the OMB Total Cost of Ownership model that is mentioned in the GAO report. OMB discontinued use of that tool in FY13. NASA respectfully requests OMB reinstate that modelling tool, until such time as an alternate tool is provided to meet the objective.

2

Recommendation 2: Direct responsible officials to report all data center consolidation cost savings and avoidances to OMB in accordance with established guidance.

Management's Response: NASA concurs. NASA will issue the required directive by October 31, 2014.

Thank you for the opportunity to comment on this draft report. If you have any questions or require additional information, please contact Ruth McWilliams at (202) 358-5125.

Larry N. Sweet

Appendix XII: Comments from the Office of Personnel Management

UNITED STATES OFFICE OF PERSONNEL MANAGEMENT
Washington, DC 20415

Chief Information
Officer

AUG 1 8 2014

Mr. David A. Powner
Director
Information Technology
Management Issues
U.S. Government Accountability Office
441 G. Street N.W.
Washington, DC 20548

Dear Mr. Powner:

The U.S. Office of Personnel Management (OPM) recognizes that even the most well run programs can benefit from an external evaluation, and we appreciate the input from the Government Accountability Office (GAO). We have reviewed your draft audit report (GAO-14-713) titled "Data Center Consolidation, Reporting Can Be Improved to Reflect Substantial Planned Savings." A specific response to your recommendation follows.

Response to Recommendation

GAO Recommendation:

We recommend that the Director of the Office of Personnel Management direct responsible officials to report all data center consolidation cost savings and avoidances to OMB in accordance with established guidance.

Management Response:

We concur. OPM is preparing its data center consolidation plan to include consideration for shared services and cloud technologies. Our data center consolidation efforts should begin in late FY14 and continue through FY15, subject to the availability of funds. Any cost savings from the consolidation will be reported once the data center consolidation plan is implemented.

If you have any questions, please feel free to contact Janet Barnes, Director, Internal Oversight and Control (202) 606-3207.

Sincerely,

Donna K. Seymour
Chief Information Officer

www.opm.gov   Recruit, Retain and Honor a World-Class Workforce to Serve the American People   www.usajobs.gov

Appendix XIII: Comments from the Department of Housing and Urban Development

U.S. DEPARTMENT OF HOUSING AND URBAN DEVELOPMENT
WASHINGTON, DC 20410-3000

CHIEF INFORMATION OFFICER

AUG 1 5 2014

Mr. David A. Powner
Director, Information Technology
 Management Issues
U.S. Government Accountability Office
441 G Street, NW
Washington, DC 20548

Dear Mr. Powner:

     Thank you for the opportunity to comment on the Government Accountability Office (GAO) draft report entitled, *Data Center Consolidation: Reporting Can Be Improved to Reflect Substantial Planned Savings* (GAO-14-713).

     The U.S. Department of Housing and Urban Development reviewed the draft report and has no comment. The Department remains committed to maximizing the value of Federal Information Technology which includes promoting the Federal Data Center Consolidation Initiative.

     If you have questions or require additional information, please contact Joyce M. Little, Chief, Audit Compliance Branch, at (202) 402-7404 (Joyce.M.Little@hud.gov) or Juanita L. Toatley, Audit Liaison, Audit Compliance Branch, at (202) 402-3555 (Juanita.L.Toatley@hud.gov).

Sincerely,

Rafael C. Diaz
Chief Information Officer

Appendix XIV: Comments from the National Science Foundation

NATIONAL SCIENCE FOUNDATION
4201 WILSON BOULEVARD
ARLINGTON, VIRGINIA 22230

Mr. David A. Powner
Director, Information Technology Management Issues
U.S. Government Accountability Office
441 G Street, NW
Washington, DC 20548

Dear Mr. Powner:

Thank you for providing the opportunity to review the draft Government Accountability Office (GAO) Report "Data Center Consolidation: Reporting Can Be Improved to Reflect Substantial Planned Savings" (GAO 14-713). We have no comments on the draft report.

NSF is committed to continual improvement in information technology management, including our efforts related to data center consolidation. We appreciate GAO's interest and work in this area.

If you require any additional information, please feel free to contact me at anorthcu@nsf.gov or (703) 292-8100.

Sincerely,

Amy Northcutt
Chief Information Officer

Appendix: XV: Comments from the Social Security Administration

SOCIAL SECURITY
Office of the Commissioner

August 11, 2014

Mr. David A. Powner
Director, Information Technology
 Management Issues
United States Government Accountability Office
441 G Street, NW
Washington, DC 20548

Dear Mr. Powner:

Thank you for the opportunity to review the draft report, "DATA CENTER CONSOLIDATION: Reporting Can Be Improved to Reflect Substantial Planned Savings" (GAO-14-713). We have no comments.

If you have any questions, please contact me at (410) 966-9014. Your staff may contact Gary S. Hatcher, our Senior Advisor for Records Management and Audit Liaison Staff, at (410) 965-0680.

Sincerely,

Katherine Thornton
Deputy Chief of Staff

SOCIAL SECURITY ADMINISTRATION   BALTIMORE, MD 21235-0001

Appendix XVI: GAO Contact and Staff Acknowledgments

GAO Contact	David A. Powner, (202) 512-9286 or pownerd@gao.gov
Staff Acknowledgments	In addition to the contact named above, individuals making contributions to this report included Dave Hinchman (Assistant Director), Justin Booth, Rebecca Eyler, Brandon Sanders, and Jonathan Ticehurst.